Aviation Maintenance Tec

ORAL & PRACTICAL EXAM GUIDE

Third Edition

Based on the original text by
Dale Crane

Edited by
Raymond E. Thompson
College of Aviation, Western Michigan University

*The comprehensive guide to prepare you for the FAA **General, Airframe, and Powerplant** Oral & Practical Exams*

Aviation Supplies & Academics, Inc.
Newcastle, Washington

Aviation Maintenance Technician Oral & Practical Exam Guide
Third Edition
by Dale Crane

Aviation Supplies & Academics, Inc.
7005 132nd Place SE
Newcastle, WA 98059-3153
asa@asa2fly.com | www.asa2fly.com

Visit the ASA website often at **www.asa2fly.com/TextbookUpdates** to find updates posted there due to FAA regulation revisions that may affect this book.

Printed in the United States of America
2019   2018   2017   9 8 7 6 5 4 3 2

ASA-OEG-AMT3
ISBN   978-1-61954-410-9

Library of Congress Cataloging-in-Publication Data:
Crane, Dale.
  Aviation maintenance technician oral & practical exam guide / by
  Dale Crane.
     p.   cm.
     "Oral & practical test for General, Airframe, and Powerplant."
     "ASA-OEG-AMT."
     Includes bibliographical references.
     1. Airplanes—Maintenance and repair—Examinations, ques-
  tions, etc. I. Title II. Title: Aviation maintenance technician oral and
  practical exam guide.
  TL671.9.C66465   1994
  629.134'6'076—dc20   94-33147
                                                      CIP

Contents

Preface   v
Certification of Maintenance Airmen   vi
The Oral and Practical Tests   x

The General Oral and Practical Tests   1

Basic Electricity   3
Aircraft Drawings   13
Weight and Balance   17
Fluid Lines and Fittings   22
Materials and Processes   24
Ground Operation and Servicing   34
Cleaning and Corrosion Control   39
Mathematics   44
Maintenance Forms and Records   50
Basic Physics   54
Maintenance Publications   62
Aviation Mechanic Privileges and Limitations   68

The Airframe Oral and Practical Tests   71

Section 1 Airframe Structures

Wood Structures   74
Aircraft Covering   78
Aircraft Finishes   83
Sheet Metal and Non-Metallic Structures   89
Welding   96
Assembly and Rigging   101
Airframe Inspection   106

Section 2 Airframe Systems and Components

Aircraft Landing Gear Systems   109
Hydraulic and Pneumatic Power Systems   115
Cabin Atmosphere Control Systems   121
Aircraft Instrument Systems   129
Communications and Navigation Systems   135
Aircraft Fuel Systems   139
Aircraft Electrical Systems   145
Position and Warning System   151
Ice and Rain Control Systems   154
Fire Protection Systems   158

The Powerplant Oral and Practical Tests 165

Reciprocating Engines   167
Turbine Engines   171
Engine Inspection   173
Engine Instrument Systems   175
Engine Fire Protection Systems   179
Engine Electrical Systems   182
Lubrication Systems   185
Ignition and Starting Systems   189
Fuel Metering Systems   194
Engine Fuel Systems   196
Induction and Engine Airflow Systems   199
Engine Cooling Systems   201
Engine Exhaust and Thrust Reverser Systems   203
Propellers   205
Turbine-Powered Auxiliary Power Units   211

Preface

Certification as an aviation mechanic is a major step in your career. You were required to have a certain level of experience to qualify to take your knowledge tests, and having passed all sections, you are now ready for the final step, the oral and practical tests.

The knowledge tests are strictly objective and verify only your knowledge of facts. When taking them, you are interfacing with a computer and there is no personal involvement.

The oral and practical tests are different. In these you work directly with an experienced mechanic on a one-on-one basis. This examiner is able to not only judge your mechanical skills, but to observe the way you think and see the way you solve problems.

It is important that you approach the oral and practical tests with the proper mental attitude. The examiner has one basic thought in mind, that of determining whether or not you have the level of skill needed for an entry-level technician. The examiner will not try to trick you in any way, and he or she wants you to pass almost as much as you do.

If you are asked a question to which you do not know the answer, admit it rather than try to bluff your way through. If you are given a project that you do not understand, discuss it with the examiner. Especially, don't bungle your way through a project you cannot properly execute. The examiner will discuss the project with you, but will show little or no tolerance for your driving ahead with a project you obviously cannot handle.

The oral and practical tests are your last steps toward certification, so study this guide carefully as it is designed to help you prepare for them. We wish you success with them.

Dale Crane
2000

Preface to the Third Edition

The oral and practical exam process has changed radically in recent years. The core practical test items have been removed and the oral and practical questions and projects are randomly generated. This means that examiners must be prepared to test on all projects and students able to perform on all projects.

This also means that the number of practical projects is greatly increased. There are a number of new projects as well; these projects are defined by the Practical Test Standards (PTS) and are captured in this Third Edition. Some test areas were eliminated and new sections added to reflect changes to the PTS.

Raymond E. Thompson, Technical Editor
College of Aviation
Western Michigan University
2016

Certification of Maintenance Airmen

The Federal Aviation Administration has three classifications of maintenance airmen: repairman, authorized inspector, and mechanic. Certification in each category has special requirements and special privileges. This *Oral & Practical Exam Guide* applies to the tests for mechanic certification, but all three classifications are described below.

Repairman

The applicant for a repairman certificate must be employed for a specific job requiring his or her special qualifications by a certificated commercial operator or certificated air carrier.

A repairman applicant must have at least 18 months of practical experience in the procedures, practices, inspection methods, materials, tools, machine tools, and equipment generally used in the maintenance duties of the specific job for which he or she is to be employed and certificated. Or, the applicant must have completed specialized formal training that is acceptable to the administrator and specifically designed to qualify the applicant for the job for which he or she is to be employed.

A repairman may exercise the privileges of the certificate only in connection with the duties for the certificate holder by whom the repairman was certificated and recommended.

There is a special type of repairman certificate issued to the builder of an experimental aircraft which allows the holder to perform condition inspections on the aircraft constructed by him or her.

Authorized Inspector

An applicant for an inspection authorization (IA) must:

- Hold a currently effective mechanic certificate with both an airframe and a powerplant rating that has been in effect for a total of at least 3 years.
- Have been actively engaged, for at least the 2-year period before the date of application, in maintaining civil certificated aircraft.
- Have a fixed base of operation.
- Have available the equipment, facilities, and inspection data necessary to properly inspect airframes, powerplants, propellers, or any related part or appliance.
- Pass a knowledge test on his or her ability to inspect according to safety standards for returning aircraft to service after major repairs and major alterations, and annual and progressive inspections performed under 14 CFR Part 43.

The holder of an inspection authorization may:

- Inspect and approve for return to service an aircraft after a major repair or major alteration if the work has been done in accordance with technical data that has been approved by the administrator.
- Perform an annual inspection, or perform or supervise a progressive inspection.

An inspection authorization expires on March 31 of each year and must be renewed for a 1-year period at that time.

Mechanic

The FAA issues a Mechanic Certificate with an Airframe rating, Powerplant rating, or both ratings to applicants who are properly qualified. Below are descriptions of the experience, knowledge, and practical requirements, and suggested study references for all three ratings.

Requirements for Mechanic Certification

14 CFR Part 65 *Certification: Airmen Other Than Flight Crewmembers* covers the requirements for mechanic certification, described below.

Basic Requirements

- Must be at least 18 years of age.

- Must be able to read, write, speak, and understand the English language, or in the case of an applicant who does not meet this requirement and who is employed outside of the United States by a U.S. air carrier, have his or her certificate endorsed "Valid only outside the United States."

- Must have passed all of the prescribed tests within a period of 24 months.

Experience Requirements

Must have a graduation certificate or certificate of completion from a certificated aviation maintenance technician school, or documentary evidence, satisfactory to the Administrator, of:

- At least 18 months of practical experience with the procedures, practices, materials, tools, machine tools, and equipment generally used in constructing, maintaining, or altering airframes or powerplants appropriate to the rating sought; or

- At least 30 months of practical experience concurrently performing the duties appropriate to both the airframe and powerplant ratings.

Knowledge Requirements and Knowledge Tests

After meeting the applicable experience requirements, each applicant for a mechanic certificate must pass a knowledge test covering the construction and maintenance of aircraft appropriate to the rating sought, the regulations that pertain to the rating, and the applicable provisions of 14 CFR Part 43 (*Maintenance, Preventive Maintenance, Rebuilding, and Alteration*) and Part 91 (*General Operating and Flight Rules*).

The basic principles covering the installation and maintenance of propellers are included in the powerplant test.

The applicant must pass each section of the knowledge test before applying for the oral and practical tests. There are three knowledge tests, a General test that is required for both ratings, and tests for both the Airframe and Powerplant ratings. An applicant for the Airframe rating must pass the General and the Airframe test, and an applicant for the Powerplant rating must pass the General and Powerplant test. The General test needs to be taken only one time.

All test questions are the objective, multiple-choice type with three choices of answers. The minimum passing grade for each test is 70 percent.

The General test consists of 60 multiple-choice questions selected by computer from more than 600 questions in the *Aviation Mechanic—General* test question bank. You are allowed 1.5 hours to take this test. The Airframe and Powerplant tests each consist of 100 multiple-choice questions taken from the more than 1,000-question *Aviation Mechanic—Airframe* and the more than 1,000-question *Aviation Mechanic—Powerplant* test question banks. You are allowed 2 hours for each of these tests.

If the score on your airman test report is 70 or above, the report is valid for 24 calendar months. You may elect to retake the test in anticipation of a better score, after 30 days from the date your test was taken. The score of the latest test you take will become the official test score. If you fail a knowledge test, you may apply for retesting before 30 days if you present the failed test report and an endorsement from an authorized mechanic certificate holder. This endorsement must certify that additional instruction has been given, and you have been found competent to pass the test (the endorsement is not necessary if you wait 30 days).

Skill Requirements

Each applicant for a mechanic certificate or rating must pass an oral and a practical test on the rating sought. These tests cover the applicant's basic skill in performing practical projects on the subjects covered by the knowledge test for that rating. These testing procedures are covered in detail beginning on Page x.

An applicant for a Powerplant rating must show his or her ability to make satisfactory minor repairs to, and minor alterations of propellers.

The examiner will download an oral and practical examination that is generated at random for each applicant. Each candidate should be familiar with all the knowledge and skill requirements contained within the appropriate test standards.

ASA Study Materials

The ASA Fast-Track Guides for General, Airframe, and Powerplant Mechanic have been specially prepared to help you get ready to take your FAA knowledge tests, and since the same material is covered in your oral and practical tests, review all of the questions and answers in the knowledge test portion of these Guides.

The questions in this Exam Guide are typical of those you will likely be asked. The practical projects that accompany each section are typical of those the examiner will be apt to use to check your level of skill. The *actual* questions and projects will depend upon the examiner. Your examiner is a knowledgeable mechanic who can evaluate your capabilities, so don't try to "snow" him or her with words when you don't know the answer, and don't attempt any project that you are not competent to handle. It is far better to admit your lack of knowledge or skill than to blunder into a project, which shows that you lack the judgment to properly evaluate your capabilities.

Included in each section of this Guide are references to other ASA textbooks, FAA handbooks and Advisory Circulars, and other study materials that apply specifically to that section or subject covered, such as manufacturers' service guides and information.

Reference codes used in this guide are as follows:

AMT-G	*Aviation Maintenance Technician—General* (ASA)
AMT-STRUC	*Aviation Maintenance Technician—Airframe, Volume 1* (ASA)
AMT-SYS	*Aviation Maintenance Technician—Airframe, Volume 2* (ASA)
AMT-P	*Aviation Maintenance Technician—Powerplant* (ASA)
ASA-MHB	*Aviation Mechanic Handbook* (ASA)
FAA-S-8081-26, -27, -28	Aviation Mechanic for General, Airframe, and Powerplant Practical Test Standards (available as ASA-8081-AMT)
AC 39-7	Airworthiness Directives (FAA Advisory Circular)
AC 65-2	Airframe and Powerplant Mechanic's Certification Guide (FAA Advisory Circular)
AC 43-4A	Corrosion Control for Aircraft (FAA Advisory Circular)
AC 43.13-1B	Acceptable Methods, Techniques, and Practices—Aircraft Inspection and Repair (FAA Advisory Circular)
14 CFR	Title 14 of the Code of Federal Regulations. (Reprints of the applicable parts are in ASA's FAR/AMT.)

The Oral and Practical Tests

Prerequisites

All applicants must have met the prescribed experience requirements as stated in 14 CFR §65.77. In addition, all applicants must provide:

1. Proof of having unexpired passing credit for the Aviation Mechanic General (AMG) knowledge test by presenting an Airman Computer Test Report (except when properly authorized under the provisions of 14 CFR §65.80 to take the practical tests before the airman knowledge tests).

2. Identification with a photograph and signature.

Test Standards

The examiner will download an oral and practical examination that is generated at random for each applicant that reflects all the knowledge and skill "Areas of Operation."

"Areas of Operation" are subject areas in which aviation mechanic applicants must have knowledge or demonstrate skill.

"Tasks" are the items that should be performed according to standards acceptable to the examiner.

"Reference" identifies the publication(s) that describe the task. *Information contained in manufacturer and/or FAA approved data always takes precedence over textbook referenced data.*

The objective of each Task lists the elements that must be satisfactorily performed to demonstrate competency in the Task.

The objective includes:

1. Specifically what the applicant will be able to do.

2. Conditions under which the Task is to be performed.

3. Acceptable standards of performance.

These terms apply to each Task:

- "Inspect" means to examine by sight and touch.
- "Check" means to verify proper operation.
- "Troubleshoot" means to analyze and identify malfunctions.
- "Service" means to perform functions that ensure continued operation.
- "Repair" means to correct a defective condition.
- "Overhaul" means to disassemble, inspect, repair as necessary, and check.

The applicant should be well prepared in *all* knowledge and skill areas included in the standards.

Satisfactory performance to meet the requirements for certification is based on the applicant's ability to:

1. Show basic knowledge.
2. Demonstrate basic mechanic skills.
3. Perform the Tasks within the standards of the reference materials.

The practical test is passed if, in the judgment of the examiner, the applicant demonstrates the prescribed level of proficiency on the assigned Tasks in each Area of Operation. Each practical examination item must be performed, at a minimum, to the performance level in the practical test standards. For mechanic testing, there are three practical performance levels:

- Level 1: You must know basic facts and principles and be able to locate information and reference materials. You do not have to interpret information or demonstrate a physical skill.

- Level 2: Know and understand principles, theories, operations, and concepts. You must be able to find, interpret, and apply maintenance data and information. You must be able to select and utilize the appropriate tools and equipment. While you need to demonstrate adequate performance skills, you do not need to demonstrate skill at a high or return-to-service quality level.

- Level 3: Know and understand principles, theories, operations, and concepts. You must be able to find, interpret, and apply maintenance data and information, select and utilize the appropriate tools and equipment to the overall operation and maintenance of an aircraft. You must be able to demonstrate the ability to work independently and make accurate judgments of airworthiness. You must demonstrate skills at a high level which includes the ability to perform return-to-service levels of work.

If, in the judgment of the examiner, the applicant does not meet the standards of any Task performed, the associated Area of Operation is failed and therefore, the practical test is failed.

Typical areas of unsatisfactory performance and grounds for disqualification are:

1. Any action or lack of action by the applicant that requires corrective intervention by the examiner for reasons of safety.
2. Failure to follow recommended maintenance practices and/or reference material while performing projects.
3. Exceeding tolerances stated in the reference material.
4. Failure to recognize improper procedures.
5. The inability to perform to a return-to-service standard, where applicable.
6. Inadequate knowledge in any of the subject areas.

When an applicant fails a test the examiner will record the applicant's unsatisfactory performance and Tasks not completed in terms of Areas of Operation appropriate to the practical test conducted.

The General Oral and Practical Tests

There are twelve "Areas of Operation" that are tested on the General Oral and Practical Exams.

Following this list are the suggested study areas, typical oral questions with succinct answers and typical practical projects for each area of operation.

I. Basic Electricity
   A: Measure capacitance
   B: Calculate inductance
   C: Calculate and measure electrical power
   D: Measure voltage, current, resistance, and continuity
   E: Determine the relationship of voltage, current, and resistance in electrical circuits
   F: Read and interpret aircraft electrical circuit diagrams, including solid state devices and logic functions.
   G: Inspect and service lead-acid batteries
   H: Inspect and service nickel-cadmium batteries

II. Aircraft Drawings
   A: Use drawings, symbols, and system schematics
   B: Draw sketches of repairs and alterations
   C: Use blueprint information
   D: Use graphs and charts

III. Weight and Balance
   A: Weigh aircraft
   B: Perform weight and balance check and record data

IV. Fluid Lines and Fittings
   A: Fabricate and install rigid fluid lines and fittings
   B: Fabricate and install flexible fluid lines and fittings

V. Materials and Processes
   A: Identify and select appropriate nondestructive testing methods
   B: Perform dye penetrant, eddy current, ultrasonic, or magnetic particle inspections
   C: Perform basic heat-treating processes
   D: Identify and select aircraft solid shank rivets, bolts, and associated hardware
   E: Identify and select aircraft materials
   F: Inspect welds
   G: Perform precision measurements

VI. Ground Operation and Servicing
   A: Start, ground operate, and move aircraft and identity typical ground operation hazards
   B: Service aircraft
   C: Secure aircraft
   D: Identify and select fuels

Continued

VII. Cleaning and Corrosion Control
   A: Identify and select cleaning materials
   B: Inspect and identify aircraft corrosion
   C: Remove and treat aircraft corrosion and perform aircraft cleaning
   D: Clean and protect metallic materials
   E: Clean and protect plastics and composite materials

VIII. Mathematics
   A: Extract roots and raise numbers to a given power
   B: Determine areas and volumes of various geometrical shapes
   C: Solve ratio, proportion, and percentage problems
   D: Perform algebraic operations involving addition, subtraction, multiplication, and division of positive and negative numbers

IX. Maintenance Forms and Records
   A: Write descriptions of work performed, including aircraft discrepancies and corrective actions using typical aircraft maintenance records
   B: Complete required maintenance forms, records, and inspection reports
   C: FAA forms and information

X. Basic Physics
   A: Use and understand the principles of simple machines and sound dynamics
   B: Use and understand the principles of fluid dynamics
   C: Use and understand the principles of heat dynamics
   D: Use and understand the principles of basic aerodynamics, aircraft structures, and theory of flight

XI. Maintenance Publications
   A: Demonstrate ability to read, comprehend, and apply information contained in FAA and manufacturer's aircraft maintenance specifications and data sheets
   B: Demonstrate ability to read, comprehend, and apply information contained in aircraft maintenance manuals, and related publications
   C: Demonstrate ability to read, comprehend, and apply information contained in Federal Aviation Regulations
   D: Demonstrate ability to read, comprehend, and apply information contained in Airworthiness Directives (AD)s
   E: Demonstrate ability to read, comprehend, and apply information contained in advisory material

XII. Aviation Mechanic Privileges and Limitations
   A: Exercise mechanic privileges within the limitations prescribed by 14 CFR Part 65

I. Area of Operation: Basic Electricity
A. Task: Measure Capacitance

Reference: AMT-G, Chapter 4

Typical Oral Questions

1. **What constitutes a capacitor?**
   Two conductors separated by an insulator.

2. **What is the purpose of a capacitor?**
   It stores electrical energy in electrostatic fields.

3. **Does a capacitor in an AC circuit cause the current to lead or lag the voltage?**
   It causes the current to lead the voltage.

4. **What is the basic unit of capacitance?**
   The farad.

5. **Why should electrolytic capacitors not be used in an AC circuit?**
   They are polarized. An electrolytic capacitor will pass current of one polarity, but will block current of the opposite polarity.

Typical Practical Projects

1. Using a capacitor tester and capacitor furnished by the examiner, determine the capacity of a capacitor and whether or not it is serviceable.

2. Find the capacitive reactance in an AC circuit for the values of capacitance and frequency specified by the examiner.

B. Task: Calculate Inductance

Reference: AMT-G, Chapter 4

Typical Oral Questions

1. **What is meant by inductance?**
   The ability to store electrical energy in electromagnetic fields.

2. **What is the basic unit of inductance?**
   The henry.

3. What is an example of an inductor used in a magneto?
The coil.

4. Does an inductor in an AC circuit cause the current to lead or lag the voltage?
It causes the current to lag behind the voltage.

5. How can you find the polarity of an electromagnet?
Hold the electromagnet in your left hand with your fingers encircling the coil in the direction electrons flow (from negative to positive). Your thumb will point to the north pole of the electromagnet.

6. What is meant by impedance?
The total opposition to the flow of alternating current. It is the vector sum of resistance, capacitive reactance, and inductive reactance.

7. In what units is impedance measured?
In ohms.

Typical Practical Projects

1. Given the inductive reactance caused by a coil and the frequency of the AC in a circuit, compute the inductance.

2. Find the inductive reactance in an AC circuit for the values of inductance and frequency specified by the examiner.

C. Task: Calculate and Measure Electrical Power

Reference: AMT-G, Chapter 4

Typical Oral Questions

1. What are five sources of electrical energy?
Magnetism, chemical energy, light, heat, and pressure.

2. What is the basic unit of power in a DC circuit?
The watt.

3. What is meant by a kilowatt?
1,000 watts.

4. What is meant by a megawatt?
1,000,000 watts.

---

5. What is the formula for power in a DC circuit?

Power = Voltage times current (P = E · I)

6. What is the relationship between mechanical and electrical power?

1 horsepower = 746 watts

7. What is meant by true power in an AC circuit?

The product of the circuit voltage and the current that is in phase with this voltage.

8. In what units is true power expressed?

In watts.

9. What io meant by apparent power in an AC circuit?

The product of the circuit voltage and the circuit current.

10. In what units is apparent power expressed?

In volt-amps.

11. What is meant by reactive power in an AC circuit?

The power consumed in the inductive and capacitive reactances in an AC circuit. Reactive power is also called wattless power.

12. In what units is reactive power expressed?

In volt-amps reactive (VAR), or kilovolt-amps reactive (KVAR).

13. What is meant by power factor in an AC circuit?

The ratio of true power to apparent power. It is also the ratio of circuit resistance to circuit impedance.

Typical Practical Projects

1. Compute the number of watts of power consumed by a 1/5 horsepower, 24-volt DC motor that is 75% efficient.

2. Compute the amps of current drawn by a 1,000-watt landing light in a 24-volt DC electrical system.

3. Find the total number of watts dissipated by two lamps wired in parallel in a 12-volt circuit, if one lamp requires 3 amps and the other 1.5 amp.

D. Task: Measure Voltage, Current, Resistance, and Continuity

Reference: AMT-G, Chapter 4

Typical Oral Questions

1. **Which law of electricity is the most important for an aircraft mechanic to know?**
   Ohm's law.

2. **What are the elements of Ohm's law?**
   Voltage E, current I, and resistance R (volts, amps, and ohms).

3. **What is voltage?**
   Electrical pressure.

4. **What is the basic unit of voltage?**
   The volt.

5. **What instrument is used to measure voltage?**
   A voltmeter.

6. **To measure voltage, is a voltmeter placed in series or in parallel with the source of voltage?**
   In parallel.

7. **What is electrical current?**
   The flow of electrons in a circuit.

8. **What is the basic unit of current flow?**
   The ampere (amp).

9. **What part of an amp is a milliamp?**
   One thousandth (0.001) of an amp.

10. **What instrument is used to measure current flow?**
    An ammeter.

11. **What two things happen when current flows through a conductor?**
    Heat is generated and a magnetic field surrounds the conductor.

12. **To measure current through a component, is an ammeter placed in parallel or in series with the component?**
    In series.

13. What is meant by resistance in an electrical circuit?
The opposition to the flow of electrons.

14. What is the basic unit of electrical resistance?
The ohm.

15. What is a megohm?
One million (1,000,000) ohms.

16. What four things affect the resistance of an electrical conductor?
The material, the cross-sectional area, the length, and the temperature.

17. What instrument is used to measure electrical resistance?
An ohmmeter.

18. How can you tell the resistance of a composition resistor?
By a series of colored bands around one end of the resistor.

19. What is meant by continuity in an electrical circuit?
The circuit is continuous (or complete) when electrons can flow from one terminal of the power source to the other.

20. What instrument is used to measure continuity in an electrical circuit?
An ohmmeter.

21. When measuring resistance of a component with an ohmmeter, should the circuit be energized?
No, there should be no power on the circuit.

Typical Practical Projects

1. Measure the voltage drop across a resistor in an energized DC circuit specified by the examiner.

2. Measure the DC current through a component specified by the examiner.

3. Measure the resistance of a component specified by the examiner and determine whether or not it is within the limits specified in an appropriate service manual.

4. Demonstrate to the examiner the correct way to check an electrical circuit for continuity.

5. Install wires into an electrical connector assigned by the examiner and test for continuity.

E. Task: Determine the Relationship of Voltage, Current, and Resistance in Electrical Circuits

Reference: AMT-G, Chapter 4

Typical Oral Questions

1. **What three things must an electric circuit contain?**
   A source of electrical energy, a load to use the energy, and conductors to join the source and the load.

2. **What are three types of DC circuits with regard to the placement of the various circuit components?**
   Series, parallel, and series-parallel.

3. **What is the name of the law that describes the relationship in an electrical circuit of voltage, current and resistance?**
   Ohm's law.

4. **What is the basic equation of Ohm's law?**
   $E = I \cdot R$

5. **What formula is used to find current when voltage and resistance are known?**
   $I = \dfrac{E}{R}$

6. **What formula is used to find resistance when voltage and current are known?**
   $R = \dfrac{E}{I}$

7. **What happens to the current in a DC circuit if the voltage is increased but the resistance remains the same?**
   It increases.

8. **What happens to the current in a conductor if the length of the conductor is doubled with all other parameters unchanged?**
   It would decrease to one half.

9. **What is the voltage across each resistor connected in parallel across a 12-volt battery?**
   12 volts.

10. **How much current flows through each of three resistors connected in series if the total current is 3 amps?**
    3 amps.

11. What is the total resistance of three 12-ohm resistors connected in series?
   36 ohms.

12. What is the total resistance of three 12-ohm resistors connected in parallel?
   4 ohms.

Typical Practical Projects

1. Find the current through each resistor, the voltage drop across each resistor, and the power dissipated by each resistor in this circuit.

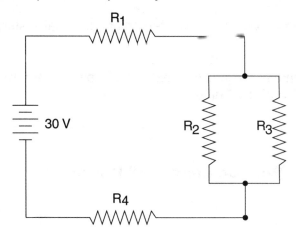

E$_1$ =	I$_1$ =	P$_1$ =
E$_2$ =	I$_2$ =	P$_2$ =
E$_3$ =	I$_3$ =	P$_3$ =
E$_4$ =	I$_4$ =	P$_4$ =

2. Using a multimeter and an energized electrical circuit, measure the voltage drop across a color-coded resistor. Compute the current flow through it and the amount of power dissipated in it.

F. Task: Read and Interpret Electrical Circuit Diagrams, Including Solid State Devices and Logic Functions

Reference: AMT-G, Chapter 4

Typical Practical Projects

1. Using an electrical schematic circuit diagram furnished by the examiner, trace the flow of current from a battery through a series of switches and relays to a component.

2. Explain to the examiner the various symbols used on an electrical system schematic diagram.

3. Using a logic diagram of an electronic circuit, explain to the examiner the function of AND, OR, NOT, and NOR gates.

G. Task: Inspect and Service Lead-Acid Batteries

Reference: AMT-G, Chapter 4

Typical Oral Questions

1. **What is meant by the capacity rating of a lead-acid battery?**
   The number of hours a battery can supply a given current flow.

2. **In what units is battery capacity expressed?**
   In ampere-hours.

3. **What electrolyte is used in a lead-acid battery?**
   A mixture of sulfuric acid and water.

4. **Does the specific gravity of the electrolyte in a lead-acid battery increase or decrease as the battery becomes discharged?**
   It decreases.

5. **What is the specific gravity of a fully charged lead-acid battery?**
   Between 1.275 and 1.300.

6. **How many cells are there in a 24-volt lead-acid battery?**
   12

7. **What is the range of temperatures of the electrolyte in a lead-acid battery that does not require a correction when measuring its specific gravity?**
   Between 70°F and 90°F.

8. **What instrument is used to measure the specific gravity of the electrolyte in a lead-acid battery?**
   A hydrometer.

9. **How do you treat a lead-acid battery compartment to protect it from corrosion?**
   Paint it with an asphaltic (tar-base) paint or with a polyurethane enamel.

10. **What is used to neutralize spilled electrolyte from a lead acid battery?**
    A solution of bicarbonate of soda and water.

11. **How high should the electrolyte level be in a properly serviced lead-acid battery?**
    Only up to the level of the indicator in the cell.

12. **Why is the closed-circuit voltage of a lead-acid battery lower than its open-circuit voltage?**
    Voltage is dropped across the internal resistance of the battery.

13. **What is the open-circuit voltage of a lead-acid cell?**
    2.1 volts.

14. **What gases are released when a lead-acid battery is being charged?**
    Hydrogen and oxygen.

15. **What precautions should be taken in the maintenance shop where both lead-acid and nickel-cadmium batteries are serviced?**
    The two types of batteries should be kept separate, and the tools used on one type should not be used on the other.

Typical Practical Projects

1. Visually inspect a battery and battery compartment for defects and provide a list of discrepancies.

2. Check electrolyte level and service as necessary.

3. Check the state-of-charge of a lead-acid battery using a hydrometer. Apply the appropriate correction for temperature.

4. Properly remove a lead-acid battery from an aircraft. Describe the proper way to clean the outside of the battery and reinstall it, correctly connecting the battery cables.

5. Properly connect two batteries on a charger for a constant-voltage charge.

6. Properly connect two batteries on a charger for a constant-current charge.

H. Task: Inspect and Service Nickel-Cadmium Batteries

Reference: AMT-G, Chapter 4

Typical Oral Questions

1. **What is the electrolyte used in a nickel-cadmium battery?**
   Potassium hydroxide and water.

2. **Why is a hydrometer not used to measure the state of charge of a nickel-cadmium battery?**
   The electrolyte of a nickel-cadmium battery does not enter into the chemical changes that occur when the battery is charged or discharged. Its specific gravity does not change appreciably.

3. **Is the electrolyte level of a nickel-cadmium battery lowest when the battery is fully charged or fully discharged?**
   Fully discharged.

4. **What is a result of cell imbalance in a nickel-cadmium battery?**
   The low internal resistance allows current to flow between the unbalanced cells and generate heat.

5. **What is a thermal runaway?**
   The large current flow allowed by the low internal resistance causes the middle cells to produce more heat than they can dissipate. The heat further lowers the internal resistance so more current can flow; this continues until the battery destroys itself.

6. How may thermal runaway be prevented?

By carefully monitoring the temperature of the middle cells and controlling the charging current to prevent an excess of current flowing into the battery.

7. How is it possible to know when a nickel-cadmium battery is fully charged?

Completely discharge the battery and give it a constant-current charge to 140% of its ampere-hour capacity.

8. What is used to neutralize spilled electrolyte from a nickel-cadmium battery?

A solution of boric acid and water.

Typical Practical Projects

1. Remove a nickel-cadmium battery from an aircraft. Describe to the examiner the correct way to clean the battery and battery compartment.

2. Check the battery for cell imbalance.

3. Perform a deep-cycling discharge and recharge of the battery on a constant-current battery charger.

4. Properly reinstall the battery in the aircraft and connect the battery cables.

II. Area of Operation: Aircraft Drawings
A. Task: Use Drawings, Symbols, and System Schematics

Reference: AMT-G, Chapter 5

1. How many views can there be on an orthographic projection?
Six.

2. How many views are used to show most objects in an aircraft drawing?
Three.

3. What information is given in the title block of an aircraft drawing?

The name and address of the company who made the part, the name of the part, the scale of the drawing, the name of the draftsman, the name of the engineer approving the part, and the number of the part (the drawing number).

4. Where is the title block normally located on an aircraft drawing?

In the lower right-hand corner of the drawing.

5. How can you know that the aircraft drawing you are using is the most current version of the drawing?

By the number in the revision block, and by the log of the most recent drawings.

6. What is a fuselage station number?

The distance in inches from the datum, measured along the longitudinal axis of the fuselage.

7. What is a butt line?

A reference line to the right or left of the center line of the aircraft.

8. What is a detail drawing?

A drawing that includes all the information needed to fabricate the part.

9. What is an assembly drawing?

A drawing that shows all the components of a part in an exploded form. A parts list is included with an assembly drawing.

10. What is an installation drawing?

A drawing that shows the location of the parts and assemblies on the complete aircraft.

11. What type of drawing is most helpful in troubleshooting a system?

A schematic diagram.

12. What is a block diagram?

A drawing that shows the various functions of a system by a series of blocks. These blocks do not include any detail, but instead indicate what happens in each block.

13. How are dimensions shown on an aircraft drawing?

By numbers shown in the break of a dimension line.

Typical Practical Projects

1. Identify the lines and symbols on an aircraft drawing specified by the examiner.

2. Using the schematic diagram of an aircraft electrical system specified by the examiner, answer a series of questions regarding hypothetical troubleshooting situations.

3. Explain to the examiner what information a selected installation diagram or schematic provides.

4. Determine the material requirements required to fabricate a part from a drawing.

B. Task: Draw Sketches of Repairs and Alterations

Reference: AMT-G, Chapter 5

1. What is the purpose of a sketch of a repair?

It shows a specific bit of information and includes the minimum amount of detail needed to manufacture the part.

2. What are the four steps in making a sketch?

Block in the space and basic shape used for the sketch.
Add details to the basic block.
Darken lines that are to show up as visible lines in the finished sketch.
Add dimensions and any other information that will make the sketch more usable.

3. What is the purpose of a center line on an aircraft drawing?

It divides a part into symmetrical halves.

Typical Practical Projects

   1. Identify each of these lines that are commonly used on an aircraft drawing.

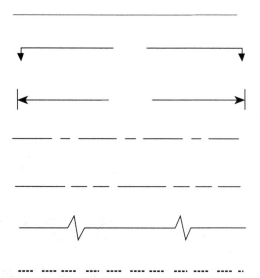

   2. Draw a sketch of a repair or alteration specified by the examiner. Use the necessary drafting tools, such as dividers, compass, ruler, T-square, etc.

C. Task: Use Blueprint Information

Reference: AMT-G, Chapter 5

Typical Practical Projects

1. On an aircraft drawing specified by the examiner, locate the following items:
   —title block
   —zone numbers
   —notes
   —bill of materials
   —change number

2. Demonstrate to the examiner the correct way to dimension a component.

3. Draw a three-dimensional sketch of a component shown on a three-view drawing.

4. Demonstrate to the examiner your ability to assemble a component using an assembly drawing.

D. Task: Use Graphs and Charts

Reference: AMT-G, Chapter 5

Typical Practical Projects

1. Using a performance chart for a specific aircraft engine, find the brake horsepower developed when the RPM and BMEP are known.

2. Using the electrical wire chart in AC 43.13-1B Page 11-23, find the wire size needed to carry 20 amps of current for 30 feet in a 28-volt circuit.

3. Using a control cable tension chart specified by the examiner, find the proper tension for a 3/16, 7 x 19 cable when the aircraft temperature is 80°F.

4. Demonstrate to the examiner the way to trace a procedure using a logic flow chart.

III. Area of Operation: Weight and Balance
A. Task: Weigh Aircraft

Reference: AMT-G, Chapter 6

Typical Oral Questions

1. **When should an aircraft be reweighed?**

   After an extensive repair or alteration that could change its weight or center of gravity.

2. **Why is it necessary to consider the category under which an aircraft is licensed when computing its weight and balance?**

   Different categories under which an aircraft can be licensed have different maximum gross weights and different center of gravity ranges.

3. **Where do you find the leveling means that are specified for a particular aircraft?**

   In the Type Certificate Data Sheets for the aircraft.

4. **What is meant by tare weight?**

   The weight of any chocks and other items that are used to hold the aircraft on the scales.

5. **What must be done with tare weight when an aircraft is weighed?**

   It must be subtracted from the scale readings to find the weight of the aircraft.

6. **Why are the distances of all the items installed in an aircraft measured from the datum when computing weight and balance?**

   This makes it possible to find the point about which the aircraft would balance (the center of gravity).

7. **Which has the more critical center of gravity range, an airplane or a helicopter?**

   A helicopter.

8. **What is included in the empty weight of an aircraft?**

   The weight of the airframe, engines, and all items of operating equipment that have fixed locations and are permanently installed in the aircraft. Empty weight includes optional and special equipment, fixed ballast, full reservoirs of hydraulic fluid and engine lubricating oil, and unusable fuel.

9. **Where is the maximum allowable gross weight of an aircraft found?**

   In the Type Certificate Data Sheets for the aircraft.

10. **What equipment must be installed in an aircraft when it is weighed to find its empty weight center of gravity?**

    All the equipment listed in the Aircraft Equipment List as "required equipment" or as equipment that is permanently installed.

11. **What is meant by permanent ballast for an aircraft?**

    Weight that is permanently installed in an aircraft to bring the empty weight center of gravity into allowable limits.

12. **Is there a Federal Regulation requiring that all private aircraft be reweighed periodically?**

    No.

13. **What must be done with temporary ballast when weighing an aircraft?**

    It must be removed from the aircraft.

14. **What must be done to find the empty weight of an aircraft if it has been weighed with fuel in its tanks?**

    The weight of the fuel and its moment must be subtracted from the weight and moment of the aircraft as it was weighed.

15. **What is meant by minimum fuel as is used in the computation of aircraft weight and balance?**

    No more fuel than the quantity necessary for one-half hour of operation at rated maximum continuous power. It is the maximum amount of fuel used in weight and balance computations when low fuel may adversely affect the most critical balance conditions.

16. **What is meant by the maximum zero fuel weight of an aircraft?**

    The maximum permissible weight of a loaded aircraft (passengers, crew, cargo, etc.), less its fuel.

17. **What is meant by undrainable fuel?**

    The fuel that is left in the tank, lines and components when the aircraft is placed in level flight position and the fuel drained at the main fuel strainer. This is also called residual fuel.

18. **Describe the way you would find the empty weight and empty weight center of gravity of an airplane if there are no weight and balance records available.**

    The aircraft is weighed, and the empty weight center of gravity is computed. These values are recorded in new weight and balance records started for the aircraft.

Typical Practical Projects

1. Demonstrate to the examiner the correct way to level an aircraft for weighing.

2. Locate the "leveling means" for an aircraft specified by the examiner.

3. Locate the datum of an aircraft specified by the examiner.

4. Explain to the examiner the way an airplane is prepared for weighing.

5. Find the empty weight and the empty weight center of gravity of an airplane that has the following scale weights:

   Left main wheel = 1,765 pounds, arm = +195.5 inches
   Right main wheel = 1,775 pounds, arm = +195.5 inches
   Nose wheel = 2,322 pounds, arm = +83.5 inches

6. Find the empty weight and empty-weight center of gravity of an aircraft specified by the examiner.

7. Weigh an aircraft and record the scale readings, including proper handling of tare items.

8. Check the aircraft weighing scales for calibration.

B. Task: Perform Weight-and-Balance Check and Record Data

Reference: AMT-G, Chapter 6

1. What are two reasons weight and balance control are important in an aircraft?
For safety of flight and for most efficient operation of the aircraft.

2. Where is the center of gravity for most airplanes located in relation to the center of lift?
The CG is normally ahead of the center of lift.

3. What is meant by the datum that is used for weight and balance computations?
It is a readily identified reference chosen by the aircraft manufacturer from which all longitudinal locations on the aircraft are referenced.

4. What is meant by moment in the computation of weight and balance?
A force that tends to cause rotation. It is the product of the weight of an object in pounds and the distance of the object from the datum in inches.

5. How do you find the moment of an item installed in an aircraft?
Multiply the weight of the item in pounds by its distance from the datum in inches.

6. **What is meant by the arm of an item installed in an aircraft?**

   The distance, in inches, between the center of gravity of the item and the datum.

7. **Where do you find the arm of an item installed in an aircraft?**

   In the Type Certificate Data Sheets for the aircraft.

8. **What is meant by a moment index?**

   A moment divided by a constant such as 10, 100, or 1,000.

9. **What is meant by the center of gravity range?**

   The distance in inches between the forward allowable center of gravity and the rearward allowable center of gravity.

10. **What is the significance of the empty weight center of gravity range of an aircraft?**

    If the empty weight center of gravity falls within the EWCG range, the aircraft cannot be legally loaded in such a way that its loaded center of gravity will fall outside of the allowable loaded CG range. Not all aircraft have an EWCG range.

11. **Why is the empty weight center of gravity range not given in the Type Certificate Data Sheets for some aircraft?**

    The empty weight center of gravity range is given only for aircraft that cannot be legally loaded in such a way that their loaded center of gravity will fall outside of the allowable limits.

12. **What is meant by the mean aerodynamic chord (MAC)?**

    The chord of an imaginary airfoil that has the same aerodynamic characteristics as the actual airfoil.

13. **What is a loading envelope?**

    The enclosed area on a graph of an airplane's loaded weight and CG location. If lines drawn from the weight and CG cross within this envelope the airplane is properly loaded.

14. **What is meant by permanent ballast for an aircraft?**

    Weight that is permanently installed in an aircraft to bring the empty weight center of gravity into allowable limits.

15. **Where must a record be kept of the current empty weight and the current center of gravity of an aircraft?**

    In the aircraft flight manual or weight and balance records required by 14 CFR §23.1583.

Typical Practical Projects

1. Demonstrate to the examiner the way to calculate empty weight and CG in inches from the datum and as a percentage of the mean aerodynamic chord.

2. Find the new empty weight and empty weight center of gravity for this aircraft after it has been altered by removing two seats and replacing them with a cabinet, one seat, and some radio gear.

   Aircraft empty weight = 2,886 pounds
   Empty weight total moment = 107,865.78
   Each removed seat weighs 15 pounds, located at station 73.
   Installed cabinet weighs 97 pounds, installed at station 73.
   New seat weighs 20 pounds, installed at station 79.
   Radio gear weighs 30 pounds, installed at station 97.

3. Find the amount of ballast needed to bring this aircraft into its proper center of gravity range:

   Aircraft as loaded weighs 4,954 pounds.
   Aircraft loaded center of gravity is +30.5 inches aft of the datum.
   Loaded center of gravity range is +32.0 to +42.1 inches aft of the datum.
   The ballast arm is +162 inches.

4. Calculate the minimum fuel for weight and balance calculations.

5. Revise the weight and balance records of an aircraft to reflect the changes made by an alteration specified by the examiner.

6. Compute the center of gravity for a helicopter.

7. Determine the distance between the forward and aft center of gravity limits for a helicopter.

8. Locate the baggage compartment placard requirements for an assigned aircraft.

9. Calculate the moment of a specified item of equipment.

10. Revise an aircraft equipment list after an equipment change.

11. Create a maintenance record entry for a change to aircraft weight and balance.

IV. Area of Operation: Fluid Lines and Fittings
A. Task: Fabricate and Install Rigid Fluid Lines and Fittings

Reference: AMT-G, Chapter 9

Typical Oral Questions

1. **Of what material are most low-pressure rigid fluid lines made?**
   1100-1/2 hard or 3003-1/2 hard aluminum alloy tubing.

2. **Is the size of a rigid fluid line determined by its inside or its outside diameter?**
   By its outside diameter.

3. **When routing a fluid line parallel to an electrical wire bundle, which should be on top?**
   The electrical wire bundle should be on top.

4. **How can you distinguish an AN fluid line fitting from an AC fitting?**
   The AN fitting has a shoulder between the end of the flare cone and the first thread. The threads of an AC fitting extend all the way to the flare cone.

5. **How tight should an MS flareless fitting be tightened?**
   Tighten the fitting by hand until it is snug, and then turn it with a wrench for 1/6-turn to 1/3-turn. Never turn it more than 1/3-turn with a wrench.

6. **What damage can be caused by overtightening an MS flareless fitting?**
   Overtightening drives the cutting edge of the sleeve deep into the tube and weakens it.

7. **What kind of rigid tubing can be flared with a double flare?**
   5052-O and 6061-T aluminum alloy tubing in sizes from 1/8-inch to 3/8-inch OD.

8. **Of what material should rigid fluid lines be made that carry high-pressure (3,000 psi or greater) hydraulic fluid?**
   Annealed or 1/4-hard corrosion-resistant steel.

9. **What is the difference between the flare angle for aircraft and automotive fittings?**
   Aircraft fittings have a 37° flare angle and automotive fittings use 45°.

10. **What should be done to the end of a tube that is to be flared?**
    The cut end should be polished to remove any sharp edges that could cause the tubing to crack.

Typical Practical Projects

1. Make up a piece of rigid tubing that includes cutting it to the correct length, making a bend of the correct angle and radius, and correctly installing the type of fitting specified by the examiner.

2. Make a proper single flare in a piece of aluminum alloy tubing.

3. Make a proper double flare in a piece of aluminum alloy tubing.

4. Make a proper bead in a piece of aluminum alloy tubing.

5. Install a piece of rigid tubing in an aircraft, using the correct routing and approved mounting methods.

6. Install and properly preset an MS flareless fitting on a piece of rigid tubing.

7. Repair a piece of damaged rigid tubing by installing a union and the proper connecting fittings.

8. Demonstrate the correct way to repair a damaged section of high-pressure rigid tubing using swaged fittings.

9. Given examples of acceptable and unacceptable bends in rigid tubing, identify the good bends and explain the reason the bad ones are not acceptable.

10. Demonstrate the correct way to repair a damaged section of rigid tubing using AN flare fittings.

11. Identify by the color code the type of fluid carried in various fluid lines in an aircraft.

12. Identify the lines and fittings used for rigid tubing.

B. Task: Fabricate and Install Flexible Fluid Lines and Fittings

Reference: AMT-G, Chapter 9

Typical Oral Questions

1. What is the function of the lay line (the identification stripe) that runs the length of a flexible hose?

To show the mechanic whether or not the line was twisted when it was installed. The line should be straight, not spiraled.

2. **Where are quick-disconnect fluid line couplings normally used in an aircraft hydraulic system?**

   In the lines that connect the engine-driven pump into the hydraulic system.

3. **Is the size of a flexible hose determined by its inside or its outside diameter?**

   By its inside diameter.

4. **What is the minimum amount of slack that must be left when a flexible hose is installed in an aircraft hydraulic system?**

   The hose should be at least 5% longer than the distance between the fittings. This extra length provides the needed slack.

5. **What is the principal advantage of Teflon hose for use in an aircraft hydraulic system?**

   Teflon hose retains its high strength under conditions of high temperature.

6. **How much pressure is used to proof-test a flexible hose assembly?**

   This varies with the hose, but it is generally about two times the recommended operating pressure for the hose.

Typical Practical Projects

1. Fabricate a flexible hose using reusable fittings, pressure test it, and demonstrate its proper installation.

2. Given examples of correct and incorrect flexible hose installation, identify the correct installations and explain to the examiner the problems with the incorrectly installed hoses.

3. Identify the lines and fittings used for flexible hose.

V. Area of Operation: Materials and Processes

A. Task: Identify and Select Appropriate Nondestructive Testing Methods

Reference: AMT-G, Chapter 7

Typical Oral Questions

1. **What is the proper type of nondestructive inspection to use for locating surface cracks in an aluminum alloy casting or forging?**

   Zyglo or dye penetrant.

2. **What inspection method would be most appropriate for checking a nonferrous metal part for intergranular corrosion?**

   Eddy current inspection.

3. **What inspection method would be most appropriate for checking the internal structure of an airplane wing for corrosion?**

   X-ray inspection.

4. **How does filiform corrosion usually appear on an aircraft structure?**

   As thread-like lines of puffiness under a film of polyurethane or other dense finish system topcoats.

5. **What inspection method would be most appropriate for checking a steel landing gear component for stress cracks?**

   Magnetic particle inspection.

6. **What type of inspection is best suited for detecting a fault within a piece of nonferrous metal?**

   Ultrasonic inspection.

B. Task: Perform Dye Penetrant, Eddy Current, Ultrasonic, or Magnetic Particle Inspections

Reference: AMT-G, Chapter 7

Typical Oral Questions

1. **Explain the procedure to use when making a dye penetrant inspection of a part.**

   Clean the part thoroughly, apply the penetrant, and allow it to soak for the recommended dwell time. Remove all of the penetrant from the surface and apply the developer.

2. **Why is it important that all parts be thoroughly cleaned before they are inspected by the dye penetrant method?**

   Any grease or dirt in a fault will keep the penetrant from seeping into the fault.

3. **Explain the procedure to use when performing a magnetic particle inspection of a part.**

   Thoroughly clean the part, magnetize it as directed by the appropriate service manual, flow the indicating medium over the surface, and inspect it under a "black" light. When the inspection is complete, thoroughly demagnetize the part.

4. **Why is it necessary to magnetize a part both circularly and longitudinally when inspecting a steel part by the magnetic particle method?**

   To detect faults that extend across as well as lengthwise within the part.

5. Does circular magnetization detect faults that are across or lengthwise to the part?

Lengthwise.

6. Why is it important that all engine parts which have been inspected by the magnetic particle method be completely demagnetized?

If the parts are not completely demagnetized, they will attract steel particles that are produced by engine wear and will cause damage to bearing surfaces.

7. What is the principle of eddy current inspection?

A current is induced into the metal being tested by a test probe. The amount of induced current is determined by the conductivity, mass, and permeability of the material, and the presence of any faults or voids.

Typical Practical Projects

1. Using dye penetrant, inspect a part furnished by the examiner.

2. Inspect a part by the magnetic particle inspection method. Correctly magnetize the part, inspect it, and properly demagnetize it.

3. Using eddy current inspection equipment, inspect a part furnished by the examiner.

C. Task: Perform Basic Heat-Treating Processes

Reference: AMT-G, Chapter 7

Typical Oral Questions

1. Why is it important that a piece of aluminum alloy be quenched immediately after it is removed from the heat-treating oven?

Any delay in quenching aluminum alloy after it is removed from the oven will allow the grain structure to grow enough that intergranular corrosion is likely to form within the metal.

2. What is meant by normalizing a piece of steel after it has been welded or machined?

Normalizing removes stresses that are locked into the material by welding or machining.

3. Explain the way a steel structure is normalized after it has been welded.

Heat the steel structure to a temperature above its critical temperature and allow it to cool in still air.

4. Why is a piece of steel tempered after it has been hardened?

When steel is hardened, it becomes brittle. Tempering removes some of this brittleness.

5. How is steel annealed?

It is heated to just above its upper critical temperature until it reaches a uniform temperature throughout, then it is allowed to cool very slowly in the oven.

6. How is steel hardened?

It is heated to its critical temperature and quenched in water, brine, or oil.

7. What is meant by tempering steel?

The steel is first hardened; then some of the hardness is removed to relieve some of the internal stresses and brittleness.

8. What is meant by case hardening?

The surface of the metal is hardened by the infusion of carbon or aluminum nitride. The interior of the metal remains strong and tough.

9. What are two methods of case hardening?

Carburizing and nitriding.

10. How is steel nitrided?

The steel part is heated in a retort in which there is an atmosphere of ammonia (a compound of nitrogen and hydrogen). Aluminum, an alloying element in the steel, combines with the nitrogen to form an extremely hard aluminum nitride on the surface of the steel.

11. Describe the method of solution heat treatment of an aluminum alloy.

The metal is hardened by heating it in a furnace to a specified temperature and immediately quenching it in water. It is soft when it is removed from the quench, but as it ages it regains its hardness.

12. Describe the method of precipitation heat treating of an aluminum alloy.

The metal is heated and quenched, then it is returned to the oven and heated to a lower temperature. It is held at this temperature for a specified time, then removed from the oven and allowed to cool in still air. This increases the strength and hardness of the metal.

13. What is another name for precipitation heat treatment?

Artificial aging.

Typical Practical Project

1. Identify and explain the differences between heat-treated and non-heat-treated aluminum alloys.

2. Given a set of different materials, determine if they can be welded and which method is appropriate.

D. Task: Identify and Select Aircraft Solid Shank Rivets, Bolts, Seals, Rings, Gaskets, and Associated Hardware

References: AMT-G, Chapter 7; Aviation Mechanic Handbook ASA-MHB

Typical Oral Questions

1. **What is meant by an icebox rivet?**

   A rivet made of 2017 or 2024 aluminum alloy. These rivets are heat-treated and quenched, then stored in a sub-freezing ice box until they are ready to be used. The cold storage delays the hardening of the rivet.

2. **What are the two most commonly used rivet heads?**

   MS20470 universal head and MS20426 100° countersunk head.

3. **What alloy is identified by the following rivet codes: A, AD, D, DD, B?**

   A is 1100 aluminum.
   AD is 2117-T aluminum alloy.
   D is 2017-T aluminum alloy.
   DD is 2024-T aluminum alloy.
   B is 5056-T aluminum alloy.

4. **What mark on the head of a rivet identifies the following alloys: 2117-T, 2017-T, 2024-T, 5056-T?**

   2117-T recessed dot.
   2017-T raised dot.
   2024-T raised double dash.
   5056-T raised cross.

5. **What is the meaning of this rivet designation: MS20470AD4-6?**

   MS20470 = Universal head.
   AD = 2117-T aluminum alloy.
   4 = 4/32 (1/8) inch diameter.
   6 = 6/16 (3/8) inch long.

6. **What type of loading should be avoided when using a self-locking nut on an aircraft bolt?**

   A self-locking nut should not be used for any application where there are any rotational forces applied to the nut or to the bolt.

7. **What determines the correct grip length of a bolt used in an aircraft structure?**

   The grip length of the bolt should be the same as the combined thicknesses of the materials being held by the bolt.

8. **How tight should the nut be installed on a clevis bolt that is used to attach a cable fitting to a control surface horn?**

   The nut on a clevis bolt should not be tight enough to prevent the clevis bolt from turning in the cable fitting and the horn.

9. **What bolt is described by this number AN6-14A?**

   AN6 = Hex head bolt, 6/16 (3/8) inch diameter.
   14 = Length = 1-4/8 (1-1/2) inch long.
   A = The shank is not drilled for a cotter pin.

10. **What is indicated by a triangle on the head of a steel bolt?**

    This is a close tolerance bolt.

11. **What is a correct application for self-tapping sheet metal screws on an aircraft?**

    They may be used to hold nonstructural components onto the aircraft.

12. **How can you tell when a self-locking nut must be discarded?**

    When you can screw the nut onto a bolt without having to use a wrench.

13. **What is a channel nut?**

    A series of nuts mounted loosely in a channel that is riveted to the aircraft structure. You can install screws in a channel nut without having to hold the nut with a wrench.

14. **Of what two materials are cotter pins made?**

    Low-carbon steel and corrosion-resistant steel.

15. **What is the smallest size cable that is allowed to be used in the primary control system of an aircraft?**

    1/8-inch diameter.

16. **What type of control cable must be used when pulleys are used to change the direction of cable travel?**

    Extra-flexible cable (7 x 19).

Typical Practical Projects

1. Given an assortment of aircraft rivets, identify an AD rivet, a DD rivet, a D rivet, and an A rivet.

2. Given an assortment of threaded fasteners, identify a clevis bolt, close tolerance bolt, corrosion-resistant steel bolt, aluminum alloy bolt, machine screw, high-temperature self-locking nut, low-temperature self-locking nut, self-tapping sheet metal screw.

3. Properly safety wire two turnbuckles in an aircraft control system. Use the single-wrap method on one turnbuckle and the double wrap method for the other.

4. Properly safety a series of bolts that are specified by the examiner.

5. Properly install a cotter pin in a bolt fitted with a castellated nut.

6. Identify, by the number of strands of wire, a piece of extra-flexible control cable, and measure its diameter.

7. Install a swaged fitting on a piece of aircraft control cable.

8. Correctly install a Heli-Coil insert in an aluminum casting.

9. Identify proper installation procedures for a seal, backup ring, and/or gasket.

E. Task: Identify and Select Aircraft Materials

Reference: AMT-G, Chapter 7

Typical Oral Questions

1. **What is the basic wood used for aircraft wing spars?**
   Sitka spruce.

2. **What type of fabric is most widely used for covering aircraft structures?**
   Heat-shrinkable polyester fabric.

3. **What is the alloy number of the most commonly used aluminum alloy for aircraft structural use?**
   2024-T

4. **What is the alloy number of a high strength aluminum alloy that has zinc as an alloying component?**
   7075

5. **Why is it very important that the surface of a piece of clad aluminum alloy not be scratched?**

   The pure aluminum used for the cladding is noncorrosive, but the aluminum alloy below the cladding is susceptible to corrosion. If the cladding is scratched through, corrosion could form.

6. **Why is it important that a piece of aluminum alloy be quenched immediately after it is removed from the heat treating oven?**

   Any delay in quenching aluminum alloy after it is removed from the oven will allow the grain structure to grow enough that intergranular corrosion is likely to form in the metal.

7. **Explain the way a piece of aluminum alloy is solution heat-treated.**

   The aluminum is heated in an oven to the proper temperature for a specified time; then it is removed and quenched in water.

8. **What is meant by precipitation heat treatment of a piece of aluminum alloy?**

   After a piece of aluminum has been solution heat-treated, it is held at a specified elevated temperature for a period of time. Precipitation heat treating is also called artificial aging.

9. **What type of composite material is used when stiffness is the prime requirement?**

   Graphite (carbon).

10. **What type of composite material is used when toughness is the prime requirement?**

    Kevlar®.

11. **How does filiform corrosion usually appear on an aircraft structure?**

    As thread-like lines of puffiness under a film of polyurethane or other dense finish system topcoats.

12. **What is the smallest size cable that is allowed to be used in the primary control system of an aircraft?**

    1/8-inch diameter.

13. **What type of control cable must be used when pulleys are used to change the direction of cable travel?**

    Extra-flexible cable (7 x 19).

Typical Practical Projects

1. Identify by the numbers stamped on the metal which aluminum alloys are heat treatable.

2. Explain to the examiner the type of reinforcing fibers that are used when stiffness is the prime consideration.

3. Explain to the examiner the importance of ply orientation when laying up a laminated composite component.

4. Explain to the examiner the difference between a thermoplastic and a thermosetting material. Identify pieces of each type of material.

5. Examine a piece of Sitka spruce to determine if it is suitable for aircraft structure.

6. Examine a fabric-covered control surface to determine if the fabric is airworthy.

7. Explain to the examiner the way to determine if an O-ring is the proper one for a particular application.

8. Inspect a piece of shock absorber cord to determine if it has exceeded its shelf life for installation on a certificated aircraft.

9. Select the correct aluminum alloy for a specified aircraft structural repair.

F. Task: Inspect Welds

Reference: AMT-G, Chapter 7

Typical Oral Questions

1. **What determines the size of tip that is to be used when gas-welding steel?**
   The thickness of the material being welded. The size of the tip orifice determines the amount of flame produced and thus the amount of heat put into the metal.

2. **How is the welding flux removed from a piece of aluminum that has been gas-welded?**
   It should be removed by scrubbing it with hot water and a bristle brush.

3. **What must be done to a welded joint if it must be rewelded?**
   All traces of the old weld must be removed so the new weld will penetrate the base metal.

Typical Practical Project

1. Inspect a set of parts with different types of welds. Identify any defective welds and explain the reason why the weld is not airworthy.

G. Task: Perform Precision Measurements

Reference: AMT-G, Chapter 7

Typical Oral Questions

1. **What kind of measuring instrument is used to measure the runout of an aircraft engine crankshaft?**

   A dial indicator.

2. **What measuring instruments are used to measure the fit between a rocker arm shaft and its bushing?**

   The outside diameter of the shaft is measured with a micrometer caliper. The inside of the bushing is measured with a telescoping gauge and the same micrometer caliper.

3. **In what increments can a vernier micrometer caliper be read?**

   One ten thousandth (0.0001) inch.

4. **What is an advantage of a vernier caliper over a micrometer caliper?**

   The range of a vernier caliper is far greater than that of a micrometer caliper.

5. **What precision tool is used to measure piston ring side clearance?**

   Thickness gage.

6. **What precision tools are used to measure the inside diameter of a cylinder?**

   A telescoping gage and a micrometer caliper.

7. **What precision tools are used to measure the inside diameter of a small hole?**

   A small hole gage and a micrometer caliper.

Typical Practical Projects

1. Use a dial indicator to measure the runout of the crankshaft of an aircraft engine.

2. Use a telescoping gauge and a micrometer caliper to measure the fit between a shaft and its bushing.

3. Measure the diameter of a shaft to the nearest ten-thousandth of an inch, using a vernier micrometer caliper.

4. Determine the torque value for an aircraft fastener.

5. Demonstrate the proper torque techniques.

6. Check the calibration of a micrometer.

VI. Area of Operation: Ground Operation and Servicing

A. Task: Start, Ground Operate, and Move Aircraft, and Identify Typical Ground Operation Hazards

Reference: AMT-G, Chapter 10

Typical Oral Questions

1. **What special precautions should be taken when towing an aircraft that is equipped with a steerable nose wheel?**
   Be sure that the nose wheel does not try to turn past its stops. Some aircraft require the torsion links on the nose wheel strut to be disconnected when towing.

2. **What publication lists the standard hand signals used for directing a taxiing aircraft?**
   ASA-AMT-G, General textbook, page 629.

3. **What action should a mechanic take while taxiing an aircraft on a runway if the tower shines a flashing red light at him?**
   Taxi the aircraft clear of the runway in use.

4. **What type of fire extinguisher is best suited for extinguishing an induction fire in a reciprocating engine?**
   Carbon dioxide (CO_2).

5. What is proper way to extinguish an induction system fire that occurs when starting a reciprocating engine?

Keep the engine running, which will blow the fire out. If this does not work, use a CO_2 fire extinguisher directed into the carburetor air inlet.

6. When starting an aircraft engine equipped with a float carburetor, in what position should the carburetor heat control be placed?

In the Cold position.

7. What is meant by a liquid lock in the cylinder of an aircraft engine, and how is it cleared?

Oil accumulates in the cylinders below the center line of the engine and prevents the piston from moving to the top of its stroke. To clear a liquid lock, remove one of the spark plugs and turn the engine crankshaft until all of the oil is forced out of the cylinder.

8. What is the procedure if a hung start occurs when starting a turbojet engine?

Terminate the starting operation and find the reason the engine would not accelerate as it should.

9. How far ahead of an idling turbojet engine does the danger area extend?

25 feet.

Typical Practical Projects

1. Properly start, run up, and shut down an aircraft reciprocating engine.

2. Properly start, run up, and shut down an aircraft turbine engine.

3. Drain a sample of fuel from an aircraft fuel system. Check the fuel for the presence of water and identify the grade of the fuel.

4. Demonstrate to the examiner the correct hand signals to use when directing the operator of an aircraft to:
   a. Start engine number one.
   b. Move the aircraft ahead.
   c. Stop the aircraft.
   d. Emergency stop the aircraft.
   e. Shut the engine down.

5. Identify the control tower light signals that may be used when taxiing or towing an aircraft.

Continued

Typical Practical Projects *Continued*

6. Demonstrate to the examiner the correct way to clear the cylinders of an aircraft reciprocating engine of a hydraulic lock.

7. Demonstrate the correct method of securing an aircraft to the flight line tie-downs.

8. Demonstrate the correct way to hand prop an aircraft engine.

9. Properly secure an airplane for overnight storage on an outside tie-down area.

10. Jack one wheel of an airplane so the wheel can be removed. Explain to the examiner the safety precautions that must be taken.

11. Connect a tow bar to an aircraft nose wheel for moving the aircraft. Explain to the examiner the precautions that must be taken when moving the aircraft.

12. Properly connect auxiliary power to an aircraft for the purpose of starting the engine. Explain to the examiner the safety precautions that should be taken.

13. Taxi an aircraft, using the proper safety procedures.

14. Properly secure a helicopter for overnight storage in an outside parking area accounting for high wind conditions.

15. Determine the amount of fuel remaining in an aircraft.

16. List the procedures for extinguishing an engine induction fire during starting.

17. Secure a turbine-powered aircraft after engine shutdown.

B. Task: Service Aircraft

Reference: AMT-G, Chapter 10

Typical Oral Questions

1. **Why is it important that the aircraft and the fuel truck be grounded together before the aircraft is fueled?**

   Grounding prevents the buildup of static electricity that causes sparks that could ignite the fuel vapors.

2. **What information must be located near the fuel tank filler opening in an aircraft powered by a reciprocating engine?**

   The word "Avgas," the minimum fuel grade.

3. **What information must be located near the fuel tank filler opening in an aircraft powered by a turbine engine?**

   The words "Jet Fuel," the permissible fuel designations, or references to the Airplane Flight Manual (AFM) for permissible fuel designations; additionally, for pressure fueling systems, the maximum permissible fueling supply pressure and the maximum permissible defueling pressure.

4. **What should be done to a reciprocating engine fuel system if turbine fuel is inadvertently put into the tanks and the engine is run?**

   The entire fuel system must be drained and flushed with gasoline, the engine given a compression check, and all of the cylinders given a borescope inspection. The oil must be drained and all of the filters and strainers checked. After the aircraft is properly fueled, the engine must be given a proper run-up and check.

5. **What precaution must be observed regarding the tools used when servicing an aircraft oxygen system?**

   Be sure that there is no oil or grease on the tools. Pure oxygen can cause spontaneous combustion of petroleum products.

Typical Practical Projects

1. Demonstrate to the examiner the correct procedures to use when pressure fueling an aircraft.

2. Demonstrate to the examiner the correct procedures to use when defueling an aircraft.

3. Drain a sample of fuel from one of the wing tanks and from the main fuel strainer. Explain to the examiner the way to check the fuel for contaminants.

4. Check the oil supply and determine for the examiner the correct grade of oil to use.

5. Service the oxygen system of an aircraft. Explain to the examiner the safety precautions for oxygen system servicing.

6. Service a shock strut with compressed air or nitrogen. Explain to the examiner the precautions to use when working with high-pressure compressed gases.

C. Task: Secure Aircraft

Reference: AMT-G, Chapter 10

Typical Oral Questions

1. **What kind of rope is best to tie down an aircraft?**
   Nylon or polypropylene.

2. **What kind of knot is used for securing an airplane with a rope?**
   Bowline.

Typical Practical Projects

1. Demonstrate to the examiner the proper way to tie an aircraft down.

2. Demonstrate to the examiner the proper way to prepare a tied-down aircraft or helicopter for predicted high winds.

D. Task: Identify and Select Fuels

Reference: AMT-G, Chapter 10

Typical Oral Questions

1. **Why is it important that turbine fuel not be mixed with aviation gasoline used in an aircraft reciprocating engine?**
   The turbine engine fuel will cause the engine to detonate severely.

2. **What grade of aviation gasoline is dyed blue?**
   Low-lead Grade-100.

3. **What damage is likely to occur if an aircraft reciprocating engine that is designed to use grade 100 fuel is operated with grade 80 fuel?**
   Detonation will occur, leading to bent connecting rods, burned pistons, and cracked cylinder heads.

4. **What is meant by detonation in an aircraft reciprocating engine?**
   Detonation is an uncontrolled burning of the fuel in the cylinder of an engine. It is an explosion, rather than a smooth burning.

5. **What is the danger of using fuel that vaporizes too readily?**
   Vapor lock can occur in the fuel lines. This will shut off the flow of fuel to the engine.

6. What type of fuel is Jet-A?

A fuel with a heavy kerosine base, a flash point of 110–150°F, a freezing point of -40°F, and a heat energy content of 18,600 Btu/pound.

7. What are two functions of tetraethyl lead that is added to aviation gasoline?

It increases the critical pressure and temperature of the fuel, and it acts as a lubricant for the valves.

8. What documentation is required for a certificated aircraft to legally operate on automotive gasoline?

There must be a Supplemental Type Certificate for the aircraft to operate on automotive gasoline.

Typical Practical Projects

1. Fuel an aircraft using the proper grade and amount of fuel. Explain to the examiner the safety procedures that must be used for this operation.

2. Identify the different grades of aviation gasoline.

VII. Area of Operation: Cleaning and Corrosion Control
A. Task: Identify and Select Cleaning Materials

Reference: AMT-G, Chapter 8

Typical Oral Questions

1. What is used to clean transparent plastic windshields and windows of an aircraft?

Mild soap and lots of clean water.

2. What is used to neutralize the electrolyte from a lead-acid battery that has been spilled on an aircraft structure?

A solution of bicarbonate of soda and water.

3. What is used to neutralize the electrolyte from a nickel-cadmium battery that has been spilled on an aircraft structure?

A solution of boric acid and water, or vinegar.

4. What solvent is recommended for removing grease from aircraft fabric prior to doping it?

Methyl-ethyl-ketone (MEK) or lacquer thinner.

B. Task: Inspect and Identify Aircraft Corrosion

References: AMT-G, Chapter 8; AC 43-4A

Typical Oral Questions

1. **Identify the areas of an aircraft that are most prone to corrosion.**

   Battery compartment, exhaust system and exhaust trails, wheel wells, lower area of the belly (bilge), piano hinges, areas of dissimilar metal contact, welded areas, inside of fuel tanks (especially integral tanks), metal fittings under high stress, lavatories, and food service areas.

2. **Where is filiform corrosion most likely to occur on an aircraft?**

   Under a dense coating of topcoat enamel such as polyurethane. Filiform corrosion is caused by improperly cured primer.

3. **Where is fretting corrosion most likely to occur on an aircraft?**

   In a location where there is a slight amount of relative movement between two components, and no way for the corrosive residue to be removed as it forms.

4. **Where is intergranular corrosion most likely to occur on an aircraft?**

   Along the grain boundaries of aluminum alloys that have been improperly heat-treated. Extruded aluminum alloy is susceptible to intergranular corrosion.

5. **Where is dissimilar metal corrosion most likely to occur on an aircraft?**

   Anywhere different types of metal come in contact with each other, especially where moisture is present.

6. **Where is stress corrosion most likely to occur on an aircraft?**

   In any metal component that is continually under a tensile stress. The metal around holes in castings fitted with pressed-in bushings is susceptible to stress corrosion.

Typical Practical Project

1. Given samples of corroded aircraft structural materials, identify the type of corrosion. Describe the correct procedure for removing the corrosion and treating the damaged area to prevent further corrosion.

C. Task: Remove and Treat Aircraft Corrosion and Perform Aircraft Cleaning

References: AMT-G, Chapter 8; AC 43-4A, Chapters 4 and 6

Typical Oral Questions

1. **What must be done to a piece of aluminum alloy to remove surface corrosion and to treat the metal to prevent further corrosion?**
   Remove the corrosion residue with a bristle brush or a nylon scrubber. Neutralize the surface with chromic acid or with some type of conversion coating. Protect the surface from further corrosion with a coat of paint.

2. **What is used to keep corrosion from forming on structural aluminum alloy?**
   An oxide coating or aluminum cladding.

3. **How may rust be removed from a highly stressed metal part?**
   By glass bead blasting, by careful polishing with mild abrasive paper, or by using fine buffing compound on a cloth buffing wheel.

4. **How should an A&P minimize corrosion at piano hinges?**
   They should be kept as clean and dry as practicable and lubricated with a low-viscosity moisture dispersing agent.

5. **What tools are proper for removing corrosion from aluminum alloy?**
   Aluminum wool or aluminum wire brushes. Severe corrosion can be removed with a rotary file.

6. **What can be used to repair the anodized surface of an aluminum alloy part?**
   A chemical conversion coating such as Alodine.

7. **What type of device is used to remove surface corrosion from a piece of magnesium alloy?**
   A stiff hog-bristle brush.

8. **How is the inside of structural steel tubing protected from corrosion?**
   The tubing is filled with hot linseed oil and then drained.

Typical Practical Projects

1. Remove corrosion from a lead-acid battery box and treat the box to prevent further corrosion.

2. Treat the cylinders of a reciprocating engine to prevent rust and corrosion when the engine is being prepared for long-time storage.

3. Treat a piece of welded steel tubular structure to prevent rust and corrosion inside the tubing.

4. Remove the corrosion from a piece of aluminum alloy furnished by the examiner and treat the metal to prevent further corrosion.

5. Treat a piece of aircraft structure so moisture cannot reach the metal and cause corrosion.

6. Demonstrate to the examiner the correct way to remove rust from a highly stressed engine component.

7. Clean aluminum or magnesium parts with a caustic cleaner.

8. Clean an assigned area of an aircraft.

9. Locate the procedures for preparing a specified aircraft or aircraft parts for extended storage.

D. Task: Clean and Protect Metallic Materials

References: AMT-G, Chapter 8; AC 43-4A, Chapters 4 and 6

Typical Oral Questions

1. **What must be done to a piece of aluminum alloy to remove surface corrosion and to treat the metal to prevent further corrosion?**

   Remove the corrosion residue with a bristle brush or a nylon scrubber. Neutralize the surface with chromic acid or with some type of conversion coating. Protect the surface from further corrosion with a coat of paint.

2. **What is used to keep corrosion from forming on structural aluminum alloy?**

   An oxide coating or aluminum cladding.

3. **How is rust removed from a highly stressed metal part?**

   By glass bead blasting, by careful polishing with mild abrasive paper, or by using fine buffing compound on a cloth buffing wheel.

E. Task: Clean and Protect Plastic and Composite Materials

References: AMT-G, Chapter 8; AMT-STRUC, Chapter 3; AC 43-4A, Chapters 4 and 6

Typical Oral Questions

1. Explain the methods used to remove finishes from a composite material.
By light sanding or abrasive blast with plastic media.

2. What is used to clean a composite material prior to repair?
Acetone or methyl-ethyl-ketone (MEK) is commonly used. It is important to verify the solvent residue is compatible with the resin system.

3. What is the proper way to clean plastics?
Flush the plastic with clean water. Remove dirt by hand. Plastics are easily scratched and usage of rags is not recommended.

4. What is the primary purpose of a finish on a composite material?
To protect the composite structure from ultraviolet degradation.

Typical Practical Projects

1. Properly remove the finish from a piece of painted fiberglass-reinforced plastic material.

2. Remove scratches from a plastic windshield or window.

3. Apply paint to a fiber-reinforced plastic material.

VIII. Area of Operation: Mathematics

A. Task: Extract Roots and Raise Numbers to a Given Power

Reference: AMT-G, Chapter 2

Typical Oral Questions

1. **What is meant by the root of a number?**
   The root of a number is one of two or more equal numbers that, when multiplied together, will produce the number.

2. **What is the eighth power of 2?**
   256

3. **What is the square root of 4,096?**
   64

4. **What is the square of 99?**
   9,801

5. **What is the cube of 5?**
   125

6. **What is the cube root of 1,000?**
   10

7. **What is the base of this expression, 10^3?**
   10

8. **What is the exponent in this expression, 10^3?**
   3

9. **What is meant by scientific notation?**
   A method of writing very large or very small numbers using powers of 10.

Typical Practical Projects

1. Find the square and cube of a list of numbers.

2. Find the square root of a list of numbers.

3. Find the cube root of a list of numbers.

4. Write 56,000,000 in scientific notation.

5. Write 0.000 000 96 in scientific notation.

B. Task: Determine Areas and Volumes of Various Geometrical Shapes

Reference: AMT-G, Chapter 2

Typical Oral Questions

1. What is an angle?
A figure formed by two lines radiating from a common point.

2. What is meant by a right angle?
An angle of 90°.

3. What is an obtuse angle?
An angle greater than 90° but less than a straight line.

4. What is an acute angle?
An angle between 0° and 90°.

5. What is a quadrant?
One fourth of a circle.

6. What is a sector?
The portion of a circle bounded by two radii and one of the intercepted arcs.

7. What is a polygon?
A closed figure having three or more sides.

8. What is an acute triangle?
A triangle with three acute angles.

9. **What is an obtuse triangle?**
   A triangle with one obtuse angle.

10. **What is a right triangle?**
    A triangle containing a 90° angle.

11. **What is an equilateral triangle?**
    A triangle with three equal sides.

12. **What is an isosceles triangle?**
    A triangle with two equal sides.

13. **What is a scalene triangle?**
    A triangle in which no two sides are equal.

14. **What is the hypotenuse of a right triangle?**
    The side opposite the right angle.

15. **What is a quadrilateral?**
    A polygon having four sides.

16. **What is a parallelogram?**
    A closed four-sided figure in which the opposite sides are parallel.

17. **What is a trapezoid?**
    A closed four-sided figure in which only one pair of opposite sides are parallel.

18. **What is a hexagon?**
    A closed figure with six equal sides.

19. **What formula is used to find the area of a circle?**
    $A = 0.7854 \cdot D^2$ *or,* $A = \pi \cdot R^2$

20. **What formula is used to find the volume of a cylinder?**
    $V = 0.7854 \cdot D^2 \cdot H$

21. **What formula is used to find the area of a rectangle?**
    $A = L \cdot W$

22. **What formula is used to find the volume of a rectangular solid?**
    $V = L \cdot W \cdot H$

23. **What formula is used to find the area of a triangle?**
    $A = (B \cdot H) \div 2$

24. What is the significance of the constant π?

Pi (π) is the constant amount the circumference of a circle is greater than its diameter.

25. What is the value of the constant π?

π = 3.1416

Typical Practical Projects

1. Using the proper formula, find the area of a rectangle with the dimensions given by the examiner.

2. Using the proper formula, find the area of a square with the dimensions given by the examiner.

3. Using the proper formula, find the area of a triangle with the dimensions given by the examiner.

4. Using the proper formula, find the area of a circle with the dimensions given by the examiner.

5. Using the proper formula, find the area of a rectangle with the dimensions given by the examiner.

6. Using the proper formula, find the area of a trapezoid with the dimensions given by the examiner.

7. Using the correct formula, find the volume of a sphere with the diameter specified by the examiner.

8. Using the correct formula, find the volume of a cube with the length of the side specified by the examiner.

9. Using the correct formula, find the volume of a cylinder of an aircraft engine with the bore and stroke specified by the examiner.

10. Find the area of a rectangular airfoil with the span and chord specified by the examiner.

C. Task: Solve Ratio, Proportion, and Percentage Problems

Reference: AMT-G, Chapter 2

Typical Oral Questions

1. What is meant by a ratio and how is a ratio expressed?

A fraction that compares one number to another; for example, 6:2 is a ratio.

2. What is meant by a proportion?

A statement of equality between two ratios; for example, $\frac{a}{b} = \frac{b}{c}$ is a proportion.

3. What is meant by a percentage?

A fraction having 100 as the denominator. For example: $65\% = \frac{65}{100}$

Typical Practical Projects

1. Find the number that is a given percentage of another number.

2. Find the speed of rotation of the shaft of a driven gear when the gear ratio and the rotational speed of the drive gear are given.

3. Convert a list of common fractions into percentages.

4. Convert a number of percentages into common fraction with the smallest denominator.

5. Find the cost of an object when the selling price and the profit percentage are known.

6. Find the number of ounces of material A to be used with 6 ounces of material B, if the materials are to be mixed so the proportion is 6:1 (6A to 1B).

7. Compute the change in torque value when using a torque wrench extension.

D. Task: Perform Algebraic Operations Involving Addition, Subtraction, Multiplication, and Division of Positive and Negative Numbers

Reference: AMT-G, Chapter 2

Typical Oral Questions

1. What is meant by a negative number?

A number less than 0, or a number preceded by a minus (−) sign.

---

2. What steps are used to add signed numbers?
1. *Add all numbers having a plus sign.*
2. *Add all numbers having a minus sign.*
3. *Of these answers, subtract the smaller from the larger number. The sign of the answer will be the sign of the larger number.*

3. What steps are used to subtract signed numbers?
1. *Change the sign of the subtrahend (the number that is being subtracted).*
2. *If the signs are alike, add the two numbers and attach the common sign.*
3. *If the signs are different, subtract the smaller from the larger and give the answer the sign of the larger.*

4. What steps are used to multiply signed numbers?
1. *Multiply the numbers, disregarding the signs.*
2. *If the signs of the two numbers are alike, the sign of the answer is positive.*
3. *If the signs of the two numbers are not alike, the sign of the answer is negative.*

5. What steps are used to divide signed numbers?
1. *Disregard the signs and divide as though the numbers had no sign.*
2. *If the signs of the two numbers are alike, the sign of the answer is positive.*
3. *If the signs of the two numbers are not alike, the sign of the answer is negative.*

Typical Practical Projects

1. Find the sum of $(+6) + (+12)$.

2. Find the sum of $(+6) + (-12)$.

3. Find the difference between $(+6) - (+12)$.

4. Find the difference between $(-6) - (-12)$.

5. Find the difference between $(-6) - (+12)$.

6. Find the product of $(-6) \cdot (-12)$.

7. Find the product of $(-6) \cdot (+12)$.

8. Find the quotient of $(-6) \div (+12)$.

9. Find the quotient of $(-6) \div (-12)$.

IX. Area of Operation: Maintenance Forms and Records

A. Task: Write Descriptions of Work Performed, Including Aircraft Discrepancies and Corrective Actions Using Typical Aircraft (Airframe, and/or Engine, and/or Propeller, etc.) Maintenance Records

Reference: 14 CFR Part 43

Typical Oral Questions

1. **What records must be made of a 100-hour inspection before the aircraft is approved for return to service?**

   An entry must be made in the aircraft maintenance records that describes the type, the extent, and the date of the inspection; the aircraft total time in service; and the signature, certificate type, and number of the person approving or disapproving the aircraft for return to service.

2. **What record must be made of the compliance of an Airworthiness Directive?**

   An entry must be made in the aircraft maintenance records stating that the AD has been complied with. This entry must include the AD number and revision date, the date of compliance, the aircraft total time in service, the method of compliance, and whether or not this is a recurring AD. If it is a recurring AD, the time of next compliance must be noted.

3. **Where can you find an example of the correct type of write-up to use for recording a 100-hour inspection in the aircraft maintenance records?**

   In 14 CFR §43.11.

4. **What action must a mechanic take if the aircraft he is inspecting on a 100-hour inspection fails because of an unairworthy component?**

   The aircraft maintenance records must indicate that the aircraft has been inspected and found to be in an unairworthy condition because of certain discrepancies. A signed and dated list of these discrepancies must be given to the owner or lessee of the aircraft.

Typical Practical Projects

1. Prepare a maintenance record entry that approves an aircraft for return to service after a 100-hour inspection. Include a list of some allowable inoperative instruments or equipment.

2. Prepare a maintenance record entry that disapproves an aircraft for return to service after a 100-hour inspection.

3. Prepare a maintenance record entry that records the proper compliance with an Airworthiness Directive specified by the examiner.

4. Prepare a maintenance record entry that records the required tests and inspection for an altimeter system installed on an aircraft flown under Instrument Flight Rules.

5. Prepare a maintenance record entry that records preventive maintenance done on an aircraft specified by the examiner.

B. Task: Complete Required Maintenance Forms, Records, and Inspection Reports

References: 14 CFR Parts 43 and 91

1. What record must be made of a major repair to an aircraft structure?

An FAA Form 337 must be completed for the repair, and a record must be made in the aircraft maintenance records referencing the Form 337 by its date.

2. How many copies must be made of a Form 337 after a major airframe repair? What is the disposition of each copy?

At least two copies must be made. The original signed form goes to the aircraft owner, and a copy goes to the FAA district office.

3. Who is authorized to perform a 100-hour inspection on an aircraft?

A certificated mechanic who holds an Airframe and a Powerplant rating.

4. Who is authorized to perform an annual inspection on an aircraft?

A certificated A&P mechanic who holds an Inspection Authorization.

5. For how long must the record of a 100-hour inspection be kept?

For one year or until the next 100-hour inspection is completed.

6. **Can a certified A&P mechanic supervise an unlicensed person as the unlicensed person performs a 100-hour inspection on an aircraft?**

   No, a certificated mechanic must personally perform the inspection.

7. **Where can you find a list of the basic items that must be inspected on a 100-hour inspection?**

   In 14 CFR Part 43, Appendix D.

8. **What is done with the aircraft maintenance records that include the current status of the applicable Airworthiness Directives when the aircraft is sold?**

   These maintenance records must be transferred with the aircraft when it is sold.

9. **What is meant by a progressive inspection?**

   An inspection that is approved by the FAA FSDO in which an aircraft is inspected according to an approved schedule. This schedule allows the complete inspection to be conducted over a period of time without having to keep the aircraft out of service as long as would be necessary to perform the entire inspection at one time.

10. **Who is authorized to rebuild an aircraft engine and issue a zero time maintenance record?**

    Only the manufacturer of the engine or a facility approved by the manufacturer.

Typical Practical Projects

1. Prepare a Form 337 describing a major repair or major alteration that is specified by the examiner.

2. Given a list of repairs and alterations to an aircraft and engine, identify the operations that require a Form 337 to be filled out.

3. Locate in the Federal Regulations the description of the tests and inspections that must be performed on altimeter systems and on ATC transponders.

4. Demonstrate to the examiner the correct way to complete an FAA Form 8010-4, Malfunction or Defect Report.

C. Task: FAA Forms and Information

References: AMT-G, Chapter 8; AC 43-4A, Chapters 4 and 6

Typical Oral Questions

1. Which FAR specifies required maintenance records?

14 CFR §91.417 specifies you must keep records of maintenance, preventive maintenance, major repairs and alterations, and 100-hour, annual, and progressive inspections.

2. What minimum information must be contained in a maintenance record?

All maintenance entries at a minimum must include a description of the work performed, references to data acceptable to the Administrator, the date the work was completed, the name and certificate number of the person performing the work, and, if different, the signature and certificate number of the person approving the aircraft for return to service.

3. How long must major repair or alteration records be kept?

A copy of all Form 337s must be kept for the life of the aircraft.

4. What is meant by permanent maintenance records?

Permanent maintenance records are kept for the life of the aircraft and are transferred when a change in ownership occurs. Permanent records include: total time in service of the airframe, engines, propellers, rotors, the status of life-limited parts, time since overhaul on items with specified time limits, current inspection status, current AD status including AD numbers, revision dates, recurrence dates, and methods of compliance, and copies of any form 337.

5. What is a malfunction and defect report?

Malfunction and Defect Reports (FAA Form 8010-4) are a voluntary reporting mechanism to report unusual problems or weakness not associated with expected wear.

Typical Practical Projects

1. Complete a Form 337 using information provided.

2. Prepare a master AD list for a specific airframe, engine and/or propeller and determine applicability by make, model, and serial number.

3. Create a current equipment list for an aircraft, listing all equipment installed.

X. Area of Operation: Basic Physics

A. Task: Use and Understand the Principles of Simple Machines and Sound Dynamics

Reference: AMT-G, Chapter 3

Typical Oral Questions

1. **What is meant by matter?**
   Anything that occupies space and has weight.

2. **What are the three basic physical states in which matter can exist?**
   Solid, liquid, and gas.

3. **What is meant by pressure?**
   Force that acts on a unit of area.

4. **What is the standard sea level atmospheric pressure expressed in inches of mercury and in pounds per square inch?**
   29.92 inches of mercury and 14.69 pounds per square inch.

5. **What characteristic of the atmosphere determines the speed of sound?**
   Its temperature.

6. **What is meant by the fulcrum of a lever?**
   The point about which the lever rotates.

7. **Give an example of a first-class lever, a second-class lever, and a third-class lever.**
   First-class: A screwdriver being used to pry the lid from a can of paint.
   Second-class: A wheelbarrow.
   Third-class: A hydraulically retracted landing gear.

8. **What formula is used to find the amount of work done when an object is moved across a floor?**
   Work = Force · Distance

9. **What determines the mechanical advantage of an arrangement of ropes and pulleys?**
   The number of ropes that support the weight.

10. **What determines the mechanical advantage of a gear train?**
    The ratio between the number of teeth on the drive gear and the number of teeth on the driven gear.

11. What is meant by the resonant frequency of an aircraft structure?

The frequency that produces the greatest amplitude of vibration in the structure.

12. What is the principle upon which ultrasonic inspection is based?

Any fault within a material will change the material's resonant frequency. Comparing the resonant frequency of a known sound material with the material under test will indicate the presence of a fault.

Typical Practical Projects

1. Identify from a drawing of a lever furnished by the examiner, the class of lever and its mechanical advantage.

2. Find the amount of force needed to roll a barrel of oil up an inclined plane when the length of the plane, the weight of the barrel, and the height the barrel is raised are all known.

3. Using a diagram of a gear train furnished by the examiner, find the speed and direction of rotation of the output shaft when the speed and direction of the input shaft are known. Compute the mechanical advantage of the gear train.

4. Design a mechanical pulley system.

B. Task: Use and Understand the Principles of Fluid Dynamics

Reference: AMT-G, Chapter 3

Typical Oral Questions

1. What are two types of fluids?

Liquid and gaseous.

2. What is meant by the density of a fluid?

The mass-per-unit volume of the fluid.

3. What is meant by the specific gravity of a fluid?

The ratio of the density of the fluid to the density of pure water.

4. What effect does the increase in temperature of a confined gas have on its pressure?

When the volume of a gas remains constant, an increase in its temperature increases its pressure.

---

5. **What effect does an increase in the volume of a gas have on its temperature if its pressure remains constant?**

   As the volume of a gas increases with a constant pressure, the temperature decreases.

6. **What effect does an increase in the pressure of a confined gas have on its temperature?**

   Increasing the pressure of a confined gas increases its temperature.

7. **What is the difference in the fluids used in a hydraulic system and those used in a pneumatic system?**

   Fluid used in a hydraulic system is incompressible. Fluid used in a pneumatic system is compressible.

8. **What effect on density altitude is caused by an increase in air temperature?**

   As the temperature increases, the air density decreases and the density altitude increases.

9. **What effect does an increase in density altitude have on engine performance?**

   As density altitude increases, air density decreases and engine performance decreases.

10. **What effect does high humidity have on piston engine performance?**

    Water vapor is less dense than dry air and thus high humidity decreases the density of the air. The less dense air decreases engine performance.

11. **What does the specific gravity of the electrolyte of a lead-acid aircraft battery indicate?**

    The amount of acid relative to the water in the electrolyte. This is an indication of the state of charge of the battery.

12. **How much force is produced by 1,000 psi of hydraulic pressure acting on a piston with an area of 20 square inches?**

    20,000 pounds.

13. **How many cubic inches of fluid is forced out of a cylinder by a piston with an area of 20 square inches, when the piston moves five inches?**

    100 cubic inches.

14. **What will happen to the pressure of a confined gas if the temperature of the gas is increased?**

    The pressure will increase.

Typical Practical Projects

1. Using a dimensioned diagram of a hydraulic cylinder furnished by the examiner, find the amount of force exerted by a specified amount of hydraulic pressure.

2. Using a battery hydrometer, measure the specific gravity of the electrolyte in a lead-acid battery.

3. Explain to the examiner the way air flowing through the venturi of a float carburetor causes fuel to be drawn from the float bowl.

4. Determine the atmospheric density and pressure altitude.

5. Determine the density of a solid object with a specific gravity of less than one.

C. Task: Use and Understand the Principles of Heat Dynamics

Reference: AMT-G, Chapter 3

Typical Oral Questions

1. **What is meant by a temperature of absolute zero?**
   The temperature at which all molecular movement stops.

2. **What is the Celsius equivalent of a temperature of 50°F?**
   10°C

3. **What are three methods of heat transfer?**
   Conduction, convection and radiation.

4. **What is meant by the absolute humidity of the atmosphere?**
   The actual amount of water that is in a given volume of air.

5. **What causes ice to change into liquid water?**
   The absorption of heat energy.

6. **What happens inside a solid material when it absorbs heat energy?**
   The molecules within the material move faster.

7. **What is the basic unit of heat in the English system?**
   British Thermal Unit.

8. How much work will one Btu of heat energy perform?

778 foot-pounds of work.

9. What is the basic unit of heat in the Metric system?

Calorie.

10. How much heat energy is in a small calorie?

The amount of heat energy that will raise the temperature of 1 gram of water 1°C.

11. How much heat energy is in a large calorie (Calorie)?

The amount of heat energy that will raise the temperature of 1 kilogram of water 1°C.

12. What is the first law of thermodynamics?

Heat energy can neither be created nor destroyed, it can only be changed in its form.

13. What is the second law of thermodynamics?

Heat energy can only flow from a body having a high temperature to a body having a lower temperature.

14. What is an example of heat transfer by conduction?

Removal of heat from an engine cylinder by air flowing over its surface.

15. What is an example of heat transfer by convection?

The uniform heating of the air in a room by a floor heater. The heated air rises and forces the cooler air down so it can be heated by conduction.

16. What is an example of heat transfer by radiation?

The heating of the Earth's surface by heat transmitted through space from the sun.

17. Why do most metals expand when they are heated?

As heat is absorbed, the electrons move faster and expand their orbits in the molecules of the metal.

Typical Practical Projects

1. Explain to the examiner the method of heat transfer used to remove heat from an engine cylinder.

2. Explain to the examiner the way a missing intercylinder baffle can cause damage to an engine cylinder.

3. Explain to the examiner the reason engine cowl flaps are normally required to be open when operating on the ground.

4. Explain to the examiner the reason aluminum alloy must not be exposed to excessively high temperature.

5. Convert a list of Celsius temperatures into Fahrenheit temperatures.

6. Convert a list of Fahrenheit temperatures into Celsius temperatures.

7. Determine the engine horsepower for a given weight, distance, and time.

8. Calculate the expansion or contraction of an engine cylinder due to temperature change.

D. Task: Use and Understand the Principles of Basic Aerodynamics, Aircraft Structures, and Theory of Flight

Reference: AMT-STRUC, Chapter 1

Typical Oral Questions

1. **What is meant by the density of air?**
   The weight of a given volume of air.

2. **What is meant by relative wind with regard to an airfoil?**
   The direction the wind strikes an airfoil.

3. **What is meant by the angle of attack?**
   The acute angle formed between the chord line of an airfoil and the direction the air strikes the airfoil.

4. **What is meant by the critical angle of attack?**
   The highest angle of attack at which the air passes over the airfoil in a smooth flow. Above the critical angle of attack the airflow breaks away and becomes turbulent.

5. **What is meant by the stagnation point of an airfoil?**

   The point on the leading edge of an airfoil at which the airflow separates, some flowing over the top and some over the bottom.

6. **What is the difference between speed and velocity?**

   Speed is the rate at which an object is moving. Velocity is the vector quantity that expresses both the rate and direction an object is moving.

7. **What is meant by air density?**

   The mass of air in a given volume.

8. **What is meant by weight?**

   The measure of the force of gravity acting on a body.

9. **What is meant by thrust?**

   The forward aerodynamic force produced by a propeller, fan, or turbojet engine as it forces a mass of air to the rear, behind the airplane.

10. **What is meant by drag?**

    The aerodynamic force acting in the same plane as the relative wind striking an airfoil. Drag acts in the direction opposite to that of thrust.

11. **What is meant by autorotation in a helicopter?**

    The aerodynamic force that causes a helicopter rotor to spin with no engine power applied to the rotor system.

12. **What is meant by dissymmetry of lift produced by a helicopter rotor?**

    The difference in lift between the two sides of the rotor disc when the helicopter is in forward flight. The side with the advancing blade produces the greater lift because the forward speed adds to the rotor speed. The side with the retreating blade produces less lift because the forward speed subtracts from the rotor speed.

13. **What is meant by a blade stall of a helicopter rotor?**

    A condition of flight in which the retreating blade is operating at an angle of attack higher than will allow for the air to flow over its upper surface without turbulence.

14. **What is meant by translational lift in a helicopter?**

    The additional lift produced by a helicopter rotor as the helicopter changes from hovering to forward flight.

15. **What is meant by ground effect in helicopter flight?**

    An increase in lift when a helicopter is flying at an altitude of less than half the rotor span. This increase is produced by the effective increase in the angle of attack caused by the deflection of the downwashed air.

16. What is meant by ground resonance in a helicopter?

The destructive vibration that occurs when the helicopter touches down roughly and unevenly. The shock throws a load into the lead-lag hinges of the rotor blades and causes them to oscillate about this hinge. If the frequency of this oscillation is the same as the resonant frequency of the fuselage, the energy will cause the helicopter to strike the ground hard with the opposite skid or wheel. If corrective action is not taken immediately, ground resonance can destroy the helicopter.

Typical Practical Projects

1. Explain to the examiner the purpose for stall strips on the leading edge of an airplane wing.

2. Describe to the examiner the function of wing fences on high-speed aircraft.

3. Describe to the examiner the way vortex generators prevent the onset of airflow separation at high angles of attack.

4. Explain to the examiner the way flaps allow an airplane to takeoff and land at a slow airspeed.

5. Describe to the examiner the way slots and slats delay the onset of a stall to a higher angle of attack.

6. Explain to the examiner the purpose of spoilers on a jet transport airplane.

7. Explain to the examiner the way winglets reduce the effect of wingtip vortices.

8. Demonstrate to the examiner the correct way to check the angular deflection of the ailerons on an airplane.

9. Explain to the examiner the operation of a stabilator.

10. Demonstrate to the examiner the correct way to check the angular movement of the elevators on an airplane.

11. Demonstrate to the examiner the correct way to check the condition and movement of the trim tabs on an airplane.

XI. Area of Operation: Maintenance Publications

A. Task: Demonstrate Ability to Read, Comprehend, and Apply Information Contained in FAA and Manufacturer's Aircraft Maintenance Specifications and Data Sheets

Reference: AMT-G, Chapter 11

Typical Oral Questions

1. **What is a Type Certificate Data Sheet?**

   A document that sets forth essential factors and other considerations which are necessary for U.S. airworthiness certification of aircraft, engines and propellers.

2. **What are Aircraft Specifications?**

   Documents that include basically the same information as the TCDS but are issued for aircraft, engines, and propellers certificated under the Air Commerce Regulations.

3. **What document specifies the type of fuel that should be used in an airplane?**

   The TCDS for that airplane.

4. **What document would you use to find the control surface movement for a specified airplane?**

   The TCDS for that airplane.

5. **Why is it necessary to refer to the TCDS for an airplane when conducting a 100-hour inspection?**

   The TCDS includes the specifications required for the aircraft to maintain its airworthy status.

Typical Practical Project

1. Demonstrate your ability to locate the following data from a Type Certificate Data Sheet for an aircraft specified by the examiner:

   a. Maximum allowable gross weight
   b. The never-exceed airspeed
   c. The minimum grade of fuel allowed
   d. The center of gravity limits
   e. Flight control travel limits
   f. The conformity of an aircraft instrument range markings and/or placards
   g. Approved tires for installation

2. Locate the applicable supplemental type certificates for a given aircraft.

B. Task: Demonstrate Ability to Read, Comprehend, and Apply Information Contained in Aircraft Maintenance Manuals, and Related Publications

References: AMT-G, Chapter 11; and manufacturers' publications

Typical Oral Questions

1. **Who issues a service bulletin and what is its purpose?**

   It is issued by the manufacturer and used to outline procedures to make the product operate more efficiently and/or safer.

2. **May the data in an aircraft maintenance manual be used as approved data for an aircraft repair?**

   Yes. An aircraft maintenance manual is an FAA-approved document.

3. **Where would you find the dimensional tolerances for the wrist pin fit in an aircraft engine?**

   In the overhaul manual for that engine.

4. **What document would you use to find an approved repair for a damaged wing spar?**

   The structural repair manual for the aircraft.

5. **What document would you use to find the part number for a landing light bulb for an airplane?**

   The illustrated parts catalog.

6. **What document would you use to troubleshoot a malfunctioning electrical flap system?**

   The aircraft wiring diagram manual.

7. **Where would you find the empty weight of an airplane?**

   In the aircraft weight and balance manual.

8. **What FAA publication describes methods of nondestructive testing?**

   AC 43-3 Nondestructive Testing in Aircraft.

9. **What is the purpose of a minimum equipment list (MEL)?**

   An MEL permits operations with certain inoperative items of equipment for the minimum period of time necessary until repair or replacement can be accomplished.

10. **What is a master minimum equipment list (MMEL)?**

    A document approved by the FAA that lists the minimum operative instruments and equipment required for safe flight in that aircraft type in each authorized operating environment.

11. What are "Instructions for Continued Airworthiness"?

A document prepared by the operator of a helicopter and approved by the FAA that explains the maintenance that will be performed. This document is described in 14 CFR Part 27, Appendix A.

12. What is an approved flight manual (AFM) or pilot's operating handbook (POH)?

Required documents that must be carried in an aircraft that list the operating limitations specific to that aircraft and its engines.

Typical Practical Projects

1. Demonstrate to the examiner the way to locate the required service bulletins that apply to a specific aircraft or engine.

2. Demonstrate to the examiner the way to use a aircraft maintenance manual to find the procedure used to jack the aircraft for weighing.

3. Locate the dimensional tolerances allowed for piston ring side clearance in an overhaul manual furnished by the examiner.

4. Demonstrate your ability to use a structural repair manual to design a repair to a damaged wing spar.

5. Use an illustrated parts catalog to find the part number of an O-ring specified by the examiner.

6. Using a wiring diagram of a landing-gear warning system, explain to the examiner a malfunction that would prevent the system warning of an unlocked landing gear.

7. Given the weight and balance manual for an aircraft, find the empty weight and EWCG of the aircraft.

8. Using the information furnished by the examiner, find the magnetizing current recommended for magnetically inspecting a part specified by the examiner.

9. Using a copy of an MEL furnished by the examiner, show what instruments are allowed to be inoperative.

10. Using a POH furnished by the examiner, identify the minimum grade of fuel allowed for the aircraft.

11. Explain to the examiner the way to use the ATA-100 specifications for locating maintenance information for an aircraft.

12. Check a technical standard order (TSO) part for proper markings.

C. Task: Demonstrate Ability to Read, Comprehend, and Apply Information Contained in the Federal Aviation Regulations

References: 14 CFR Parts 43 and 91

Typical Oral Questions

1. Are instructions included in the Federal Regulations mandatory or optional?

They are mandatory.

2. What is the purpose of 14 CFR Part 43?

It describes maintenance, preventive maintenance, rebuilding, and alteration of certificated aircraft.

3. Who is authorized to approve an aircraft for return to service after a major repair?

An aircraft mechanic holding an Inspection Authorization.

4. Who is authorized to perform preventive maintenance on an aircraft that is not flown under Part 121, 127, 129, or 135?

The holder of a pilot certificate that flies that particular aircraft.

5. Who is authorized to rebuild an aircraft engine and issue a zero-time record?

The manufacturer of the engine or a facility approved by the manufacturer.

6. Who is authorized to approve an aircraft for return to service after a minor alteration has been performed on the airframe?

A certificated mechanic holding an airframe rating.

Typical Practical Projects

1. Explain to the examiner who is responsible for assuring that all the required maintenance is done on an aircraft.

2. Demonstrate to the examiner the part of the Federal Regulations that describes the maintenance required for certificated aircraft.

3. Explain to the examiner when a flight test is required after maintenance.

4. Explain to the examiner which aircraft require a 100-hour inspection and which ones require an annual inspection.

5. Write up a maintenance record of a 100-hour inspection on an aircraft specified by the examiner.

D. Task: Demonstrate Ability to Read, Comprehend, and Apply Information Contained in Airworthiness Directives (ADs)

References: AC 39-7 Airworthiness Directives

Typical Oral Questions

1. **What is the purpose of an AD?**

   It provides guidance and information to owners and operators of aircraft informing them of the discovery of a condition that prevents the aircraft from continuing to meet its conditions for airworthiness.

2. **What is the first step in the issuance of an AD?**

   A notice of proposed rulemaking (NPRM) is published in the Federal Register.

3. **How is information on an AD disseminated?**

   It is printed and distributed by first class mail to the registered owners and certain known operators of the product(s) affected.

4. **What type of AD may be adopted without an NPRM?**

   ADs of an urgent nature are issued as immediately adopted rules without prior notice.

5. **How is information on an emergency AD sent to the owner or operator of an affected aircraft or other product?**

   By first-class mail, telegram, or other electronic method.

6. **What publication lists all of the ADs that apply to aircraft, engines, propellers, or appliances?**

   AC 39-6 Summary of Airworthiness Directives.

7. **How can you get information on subscribing to the Airworthiness Directives?**

   Contact FAA, Manufacturing Standards Section (AFS-613), PO Box 26460, Oklahoma City, OK 73125-0460.

8. **What is the significance of the identification number 91-08-07 R1?**

   91—This AD was issued in 1991.

   08—This AD was issued in the eighth biweekly period (15th or 16th week) of 1991.

   07—This is the seventh AD issued during this period.

   R1—This is the first revision of this AD.

Typical Practical Project

1. Locate an AD specified by the examiner for a particular aircraft and answer these questions:

    a. What is the effective date of this AD?
    b. What models of aircraft are affected by this AD?
    c. What serial numbers are affected by this AD?
    d. How soon must this AD be complied with?

E. Task: Demonstrate Ability to Read, Comprehend, and Apply Information Contained in Advisory Material

Reference: AMT-G, Chapter 11

Typical Oral Questions

1. Is it mandatory that the information in an AC be complied with?

No, this information is advisory in nature.

2. With which part of 14 CFR is AC 43.13-1B associated?

14 CFR Part 43.

3. May all of the information in AC 43.13-1B be used as approved data?

No, it is acceptable, but not necessarily approved data.

4. What is the purpose of General Aviation Airworthiness Alerts?

They contain information gleaned from Malfunction and Defect Reports to warn maintenance personnel of problems that have been reported.

Typical Practical Projects

1. Using AC 43.13-1B, design a repair for a damaged bulb angle stringer in the upper surface of a wing.

2. Refer to AC 43-3, explain to the examiner the difference between X-ray and gamma ray inspection.

3. Properly complete a Malfunction and Defect Report on a problem that is specified by the examiner.

XII. Area of Operation: Aviation Mechanic Privileges and Limitations

A. Task: Exercise Mechanic Privileges Within the Limitations Prescribed by 14 CFR Part 65

References: 14 CFR Part 65; AC 65-2 Airframe and Powerplant Mechanic's Certification Guide

Typical Oral Questions

1. **What is the minimum age for a mechanic certificate?**
   18 years.

2. **What are the two ratings that can be issued to a mechanic certificate?**
   Airframe and Powerplant.

3. **How many months of practical experience is needed to qualify for the mechanic rating with both Airframe and Powerplant ratings?**
   30 months.

4. **What can be used in place of the 30 months of experience to qualify to take the mechanic tests?**
   A certificate of completion from a certificated aviation maintenance technician school.

5. **What type of experience is required to take the tests for mechanic certification?**
   Practical experience with the procedures, practices, materials, tools, machine tools, and equipment generally used in constructing, maintaining, or altering airframes, or powerplants appropriate to the rating sought.

6. **What tests are used to demonstrate that a mechanic applicant has the proper knowledge?**
   The written knowledge tests.

7. **What tests are used to demonstrate that a mechanic applicant meets the minimum skill requirements?**
   The oral and practical tests.

8. **What certificate and ratings are required for a mechanic to conduct a 100-hour inspection and approve the aircraft for return to service?**
   A mechanic certificate with both airframe and powerplant ratings.

9. **What certificate and ratings are required for a mechanic to conduct an annual inspection and approve the aircraft for return to service?**
   A mechanic certificate with an Inspection Authorization.

10. When, after making a permanent change of address, is the holder of a mechanic certificate required to notify the FAA?

Within 30 days.

11. How many months of experience within a 24-month period must a mechanic have to exercise the privileges of his or her certificate?

At least 6 months.

Typical Practical Projects

1. Demonstrate your knowledge of the contents of the following portions of 14 CFR Part 65 by writing an outline of the essential information contained in:
   a. §65.81 General privileges and limitations.
   b. §65.83 Recent experience requirements.
   c. §65.85 Airframe rating: additional privileges.
   d. §65.87 Powerplant rating: additional privileges.
   e. §65.89 Display of certificate.

2. List the types of inspections that a certificated mechanic with airframe and powerplant ratings may perform and the 14 CFR reference for each.

3. List the functions a certificated mechanic may *not* supervise.

4. Define preventive maintenance, who may perform preventive maintenance, and the maintenance record entries required.

5. Determine if a given repair or alteration is major or minor.

6. Locate change of address notification procedures.

The Airframe Oral and Practical Tests

There are 2 Sections and 17 "Areas of Operation" that are tested on the Airframe Oral and Practical tests.

Following this list are the suggested study areas, typical oral questions with succinct answers, and typical practical projects for each area of operation.

Section 1 Airframe Structures

I. Wood Structures
   A: Inspect wood structures
   B: Identify wood defects
   C: Repair wood structures

II. Aircraft Covering
   A: Select aircraft covering
   B: Apply covering
   C: Inspect and test aircraft covering
   D: Repair aircraft covering

III. Aircraft Finishes
   A: Apply aircraft registration markings
   B: Apply fabric finishing materials
   C: Apply finishes to STC'd covering materials
   D: Apply paint finishing materials
   E: Inspect finishes and identify defects

IV. Sheet Metal and Non-Metallic Structures
   A: Layout and form a U-channel or L-angle
   B: Rivet sheet metal joints
   C: Inspect and test a composite structure
   D: Repair composite structures
   E: Inspect and repair transparent plastic windows

V. Welding
   A: Gas welding
   B: Gas tungsten arc welding (GTAW)
   C: Fabricate tubular structures
   D: Soft-solder wire and connector

VI. Assembly and Rigging
   A: Install a control surface
   B: Rig rotary wing aircraft
   C: Balance flight control surfaces
   D: Jack aircraft

VII. Airframe Inspection
   A: Aircraft inspections

Airframe

Section 2 Airframe Systems and Components

I. Aircraft Landing Gear Systems
- A: Inspect and service landing gear
- B: Service a landing gear shock strut
- C: Replace brake linings
- D: Disassemble and inspect a landing gear wheel
- E: Inspect and service a landing gear tire

II. Hydraulic and Pneumatic Power Systems
- A: Remove, clean, and install a hydraulic filter
- B: Remove and install a hydraulic seal
- C: Inspect and service pneumatic power system
- D: Service a hydraulic reservoir
- E: Inspect and service hydraulic pumps and valves

III. Cabin Atmosphere Control Systems
- A: Inspect and test an exhaust heating system
- B: Inspect and operate a combustion heater system
- C: Inspect and operate a vapor-cycle cooling system
- D: Inspect and operate an air-cycle cooling system
- E: Inspect and operate a cabin pressurization system
- F: Leak test a gaseous oxygen system
- G: Replace an oxygen valve or fitting

IV. Aircraft Instrument Systems
- A: Swing a magnetic compass
- B: Replace a vacuum or pressure system filter
- C: Replace a vacuum or pressure system pump
- D: Install a sensitive altimeter
- E: Perform a static system check
- F: Check instrument systems

V. Communications and Navigation Systems
- A: Replace ELT batteries
- B: Check and troubleshoot a coaxial cable with BNC connectors
- C: Identify antennas
- D: Check an autopilot for proper operation
- E: Install a nav/com radio

VI. Aircraft Fuel Systems
- A: Inspect, service, and replace fuel system transmitters
- B: Service a fuel system strainer
- C: Drain fuel sumps
- D: Remove and install a fuel tank valve
- E: Inspect fuel tanks

VII. Aircraft Electrical Systems
   A: Replace an electrical switch
   B: Replace a circuit breaker
   C: Splice and install electrical wire
   D: Adjust a voltage regulator
   E: Inspect, check, and troubleshoot aircraft electrical systems

VIII. Position and Warning System
   A: Adjust a landing gear position switch
   B: Adjust a flap position switch
   C: Troubleshoot a landing gear warning system
   D: Repair a landing gear warning system
   E: Inspect, check, and troubleshoot brake systems

IX. Ice and Rain Control Systems
   A: Check and troubleshoot an electrically heated pitot system
   B: Replace an electrically heated pitot tube
   C: Repair a pneumatic deicer boot
   D: Rain control
   E: Inspect and check anti-ice systems

X. Fire Protection Systems
   A: Fire detection and indication systems
   B: Fire extinguisher container pressure check
   C: Troubleshoot a fire detection system
   D: Service a fire extinguisher system

Section 1 Airframe Structures

I. Area of Operation: Wood Structures

A. Task: Inspect Wood Structures

References: AMT-STRUC, Chapter 3; AC 43.13-1B, Chapter 1

Typical Oral Questions

1. **Which species of wood is considered to be the standard when comparing other woods for use in aircraft structure?**

   Sitka spruce.

2. **Why must abrupt changes in the cross-sectional area of a wooden structural member be avoided?**

   Abrupt changes in the cross sectional area of a structural member concentrate stresses and can cause failure.

3. **What is the basic difference between laminated wood and plywood?**

   In laminated wood all of the grain runs in the same direction, in plywood the grain in the layers cross the others at a 90° or 45° angle.

4. **What effect does moisture have on a wood aircraft structure?**

   Moisture causes the wood to swell and crack as it dries out. It allows fungus to develop in the wood and cause it to decay.

5. **Can northern white pine be used as a substitute for spruce?**

   Yes, but it must be increased in size to compensate for its lower strength.

6. **Which wood is more inclined to warp, flat grain or vertical grain?**

   Flat grain.

Typical Practical Projects

1. Inspect a piece of wing spar material to determine if the grain deviation is within the limits allowed for aircraft wood.

2. Given several pieces of wood, examine them for condition and for meeting the specifications for aircraft wood structure.

3. Inspect a wooden aircraft structure to determine whether or not it is in an airworthy condition.

4. Inspect a plywood aircraft structure for evidence of delamination of the plywood or for the failure of the glue joint between the skin and the underlying structure.

5. Locate instructions for inspecting wood structures.

6. Identify the protective finish on a wood structure.

B. Task: Identify Wood Defects

References: AMT-STRUC, Chapter 3; AC 43.13-1B, Chapter 1

Typical Oral Questions

1. How do you detect decay in a wood structure?

Stick a sharp-pointed knife blade in the suspect area and pry the wood up. If the wood is good, it will come up as a long splinter; if it is decayed it will come up as a chunk.

2. Are mineral streaks in a piece of structural aircraft wood reason for rejecting the wood?

No, if there is no evidence of decay in the wood.

3. How is compression wood identified?

It has a high specific gravity, it appears to have an excessive growth of summerwood, and little contrast between springwood and summerwood.

4. Is a hard knot, 1/2-inch in diameter allowed if it is in the web of a wing spar?

No, 3/8-inch diameter is the maximum allowable knot, and it must meet severe restrictions.

5. Are pin knot clusters allowable in aircraft structural wood?

Yes, if they cause only a small effect on grain direction.

Typical Practical Projects

1. Inspect a piece of wood for evidence of dry rot. Explain to the examiner what should be done if dry rot is found.

2. Explain to the examiner the way to determine the slope of the grain in a piece of wood to be used in a wing spar.

C. Task: Repair of Wood Structures

References: AMT-STRUC, Chapter 3; AC 43.13-1B, Chapter 1

Typical Oral Questions

1. **What kind of glue is recommended for making repairs to a wood aircraft structure?**

   Synthetic resin or resorcinol glue.

2. **What reference material may be used for acceptable repairs to wood aircraft structure?**

   AC 43.13-1B, Chapter 1.

3. **How is a scarf splice on a wing spar reinforced?**

   Solid spruce or birch plywood reinforcing plates are glued to each side of the spar, centered at each end of the scarf.

4. **What is the correct repair to a wooden aircraft wing spar if the wing-attach bolt holes in the spar are elongated?**

   Splice in a new section of the spar and drill new holes.

5. **What is the minimum taper to use when repairing a wood wing rib cap strip?**

   12 times the thickness recommended, 10 times is minimum.

6. **How is aircraft plywood prepared for making a compound bend?**

   Soak the wood in hot water until it is pliable.

7. **What is used to apply pressure to a glued joint when splicing a wood aircraft wing spar?**

   Cabinetmakers' parallel clamps.

8. **How much pressure must be applied to a glue joint in a piece of softwood to produce a strong joint?**

   125 to 150 pounds per square inch.

9. **What kind of repair is recommended for a hole in the plywood skin of an aircraft wing?**

   A scarf patch.

10. **What is the recommended taper for a splayed patch in a plywood aircraft skin?**

    5 to 1.

11. **What is the recommended taper for a scarf patch in a plywood aircraft skin?**

    12 to 1.

12. **Why should sandpaper never be used when preparing a scarf joint in a wing spar for splicing?**

    The dust caused by sanding will plug the pores of the wood so the glue cannot get in to form a good bond.

13. **What is the largest hole in a plywood wing skin that can be repaired with a fabric patch?**

    1-inch in diameter.

14. **Why are light steel bushings often used in bolt holes in a wood wing spar?**

    The bushing keeps the spar from being crushed when the nut on the attachment bolt is tightened.

15. **How long should a glue joint be kept under pressure when splicing a wood aircraft wing spar?**

    For at least 7 hours.

16. **Which area of a wood wing spar must not contain any splice?**

    There must be no splice under wing attach fittings, landing gear fittings, engine mount fittings, or lift and interplane strut fittings.

17. **What is done to a splice in a wood aircraft wing spar to strengthen the splice?**

    Reinforcing plates are glued to both sides of the splice.

Typical Practical Projects

1. Explain to the examiner the correct way to repair a wing spar that has an elongated bolt hole in its root end.

2. Install a scarf patch in a damaged piece of aircraft plywood.

3. Properly mix a batch of resorcinol glue and explain to the examiner the correct way to apply this glue to the wood when making a repair to an aircraft wood structure.

4. Explain to the examiner the correct way to repair a piece of aircraft structure that has been glued with casein glue when he glue has deteriorated.

5. Demonstrate to the examiner the way to inspect a wood repair for airworthiness.

6. Locate the standard repair dimensions and validate the source of information.

7. List three types of wood used in aircraft structures.

8. Identify and select aircraft quality or acceptable wood to repair an assigned structure.

9. Locate the instructions and explain to the examiner the method of inspection for a wood structure.

10. Locate the instructions for wood spar repairs.

11. Locate the instructions for rib structural repairs.

II. Area of Operation: Aircraft Covering

A. Task: Select Aircraft Covering

References: AMT-STRUC, Chapter 3; AC 43.13-1B, Chapter 2

Typical Oral Questions

1. **What reference material may be used for acceptable covering methods for fabric-covered aircraft structure?**
   AC 43.13-1B, Chapter 2.

2. **What are three types of fabric that can be used to cover an aircraft?**
   Cotton fabric, polyester fabric, and glass fabric.

3. **What paperwork must be completed if an aircraft that was originally covered with Grade-A cotton fabric is re-covered using a synthetic fabric?**

   The covering must be done according to a Supplemental Type Certificate, and a Form 337 must be executed, stating that all materials and processes complied with the requirements of the STC.

4. **What type of rib lacing cord is recommended for attaching cotton fabric to an aircraft structure?**

   Waxed linen cord.

5. **What is meant by the selvage edge of a piece of fabric?**

   It is the woven edge of fabric used to prevent the material unraveling during normal handling.

B. Task: Apply Covering

References: AMT-STRUC, Chapter 3; AC 43.13-1B, Chapter 2

Typical Oral Questions

1. **Why are some portions of the structure of an aircraft dope proofed before they are covered with fabric?**

   Dope proofing keeps the fabric from sticking to the structure when the first coat of dope is applied. The fabric normally sags enough to touch the structure before it begins to pull taut.

2. **What material is used for inter-rib bracing in a fabric-covered aircraft wing?**

   Cotton reinforcing tape.

3. **What is the preferred seam used for machine-sewing pieces of aircraft fabric together?**

   The French fell seam.

4. **Should a sewed seam in the fabric used to cover an aircraft wing run spanwise or chordwise?**

   Both spanwise and chordwise seams are permissible, but chordwise seams are preferred.

5. **What are two methods of applying the fabric to the wing of an airplane?**

   The blanket method and the envelope method.

6. **What material is used to cover the overlapping edges of the leading edge metal to protect the fabric?**

   Cloth tape.

7. **What are two methods of attaching the fabric to the aircraft structure?**

By sewing and with a cement.

8. **How are the wrinkles pulled out of cotton fabric?**

Wet the cotton with water and allow it to dry.

9. **How is polyester fabric shrunk on the aircraft structure?**

With heat from an iron.

10. **What type of knot is used for locking the stitches that are used for rib lacing on a fabric-covered aircraft wing?**

A modified seine knot.

11. **What determines the spacing of the rib lacing stitches on a fabric-covered aircraft wing?**

The never-exceed speed of the aircraft.

12. **When is the finishing tape applied to a fabric-covered wing when it is being recovered?**

After the second coat of dope has dried and the nap of the fabric has been sanded off.

13. **What is an antitear strip, and when are they required on a fabric-covered aircraft?**

An antitear strip is a strip of the same type of fabric as is used for covering the wings. It is laid over the rib between the reinforcing tape and the fabric. An antitear strip is required for aircraft that have a never-exceed speed in excess of 250 miles per hour.

14. **When are drainage grommets applied when an aircraft is being re-covered?**

They are laid into the third coat of dope, at the same time the surface tape is applied.

15. **Where are drainage grommets located on a fabric-covered aircraft wing?**

At the lowest point in each bay. It is customary to install a grommet on each side of a wing rib, on the underside of the wing, at the trailing edge.

16. **What is done to cotton and linen fabric to protect it from mildew?**

The first coat of dope used on cotton and linen fabric has a mildewcide mixed in it.

17. **How wide should the surface tape be that is used to cover the trailing edge of an aircraft wing?**

Three inches wide.

18. **Why is the surface tape used on the trailing edge of control surfaces of some airplanes notched?**

Since the edges of this tape face into the wind, it is possible that it could start to lift and form a very effective spoiler. If the tape is notched, it will tear off at a notch.

19. What is the purpose of the reinforcing tape used between the fabric and the rib lacing on an aircraft wing?

The reinforcing tape keeps the rib lacing cord from pulling through the fabric.

Typical Practical Projects

1. Locate the instructions for the proper way to stitch fabric to an aircraft wing.

2. Locate the instructions for the installation of a drainage grommet on the trailing edge of a fabric-covered aircraft wing.

3. Explain to the examiner the correct procedure for covering an aircraft wing with polyester synthetic fabric.

4. Locate the instructions for the proper splice knot to use when joining pieces of waxed rib lacing cord.

5. Locate the instructions for the correct spacing to use for rib lacing on an aircraft specified by the examiner.

6. Explain to the examiner the correct way of removing wrinkles from cotton fabric that is installed on an aircraft structure before the dope is applied.

7. Identify the different types of material used in aircraft covering.

8. Identify and locate the fabric critical areas.

C. Task: Inspect and Test Aircraft Covering

References: AMT-STRUC, Chapter 3; AC 43.13-1B, Chapter 2

Typical Oral Questions

1. What is the minimum strength to which aircraft fabric is allowed to deteriorate before it is considered to be unairworthy?

Fabric can deteriorate to 70% of the strength of the fabric required for the aircraft.

2. How is the strength of the fabric on an aircraft structure determined?

An approximate strength test can be made with an FAA-approved fabric punch tester, but the only way to know for sure that the fabric has sufficient strength is by pull-testing a one-inch-wide sample of the fabric.

Typical Practical Projects

1. Locate the instructions on how to test fabric on an aircraft structure to determine if it is airworthy.

2. Determine what repairs are needed for a given damaged fabric covered structure.

3. Locate and explain fabric inspection procedures.

D. Task: Repair Aircraft Covering

References: AMT-STRUC, Chapter 3; AC 43.13-1B, Chapter 2

Typical Oral Questions

1. **What is the recommended type of repair to a fabric-covered aircraft surface when it has an L-shaped tear, with each of the legs of the tear more than 14 inches long?**
   If the never-exceed speed of the aircraft is less than 150 miles per hour, a doped-on repair can be made.

2. **What type of hand-sewing stitch is used when sewing in a panel of new fabric on an aircraft fabric-covered wing?**
   A baseball stitch, locked every eight to ten stitches.

Typical Practical Projects

1. Make a doped-on patch to a damaged area in a fabric-covered aircraft structure.

2. Demonstrate to the examiner the proper way to sew a piece of new fabric to a piece of damaged fabric on an aircraft structure.

3. Determine whether installing a Supplemental Type Certificate (STC) covering is applicable to a given aircraft.

4. Locate and explain how to repair trailing edge fabric damage.

III. Area of Operation: Aircraft Finishes

A. Task: Apply Aircraft Registration Markings

References: AMT-STRUC, Chapter 3; 14 CFR Part 45

Typical Oral Questions

1. **Where are the registration marks required to be placed on a fixed-wing aircraft?**
   On a vertical tail surface or on the side of the fuselage.

2. **What is the generally required dimensions of the registration numbers on the side of a fixed-wing aircraft?**
   12-inches tall and 2/3 as wide as they are high. The letters M and W may be as wide as they are high. The numeral 1 is 1/6 as wide as it is high.

3. **What is the regulation regarding the color of the registration marks?**
   The color must contrast with the background and be legible.

Typical Practical Projects

1. Explain to the examiner the correct size and location for the identification numbers that are required on an aircraft.

2. Demonstrate the way to lay out the registration marks that are specified by the examiner.

B. Task: Apply Fabric Finishing Materials

Reference: AMT-STRUC, Chapter 3

Typical Oral Questions

1. **Why should wooden wing spars be finished with a transparent varnish?**
   The transparent finish allows any decay or rot that develops in the wood to be detected.

2. **Why is retarder used in dope when the dope is being sprayed in humid conditions?**
   The retarder slows the drying of the dope and keeps it from blushing.

3. **When an aircraft is being recovered, when is fungicidal dope applied to the fabric?**
   With the first coat of dope that is brushed into the fabric.

---

4. **What will happen if dope is sprayed over an enameled surface?**

   The thinner in the dope will penetrate the enamel surface and cause it to swell.

5. **What are the two basic types of dope used on fabric-covered aircraft?**

   Nitrate dope and butyrate (cellulose acetate butyrate, or CAB) dope.

6. **What kind of dope is used on polyester synthetic fabric that has been heat-shrunk on an aircraft structure?**

   Nontautening butyrate dope.

7. **Why are some portions of the structure of an aircraft dope proofed before they are covered with fabric?**

   Dope proofing keeps the fabric from sticking to the structure when the first coat of dope is applied. The fabric normally sags enough to touch the structure before it begins to pull taut.

8. **What is meant by dope blushing, and what causes it?**

   Blushing is a condition in dope finished in which moisture from the atmosphere condenses on the surface and causes some of the cellulose to precipitate from the finish. Blushing leaves a porous, dull, and weak finish.

   Blushing may be caused by the temperature being too low, the humidity being too high, or by drafts or sudden changes in the temperature.

9. **What can be done to remedy blushing that has formed on a doped surface that has just been sprayed?**

   Spray a very light mist coat of a mixture of one part retarder to two parts of thinner over the blushed area. Allow it to dry and spray on another coat. If this does not remove the blush, the blushed dope will have to be sanded off and new dope applied.

10. **What is a rejuvenator?**

    A slow-drying finishing material that has potent solvents and plasticizers that soften a dried surface film and restore resilience to the film.

11. **Does rejuvenator restore strength to the fabric?**

    No, it only restores resilience to the finish.

12. **Why is the first coat of dope brushed onto the fabric?**

    To ensure thorough penetration and encapsulation of all of the fibers.

13. **What is the general reason for runs and sags in a finish that is being sprayed onto a flat surface?**

    Too much dope is being applied. The film is too thick.

14. **What is the most common cause for dope roping?**

    The dope was improperly thinned or it was too cold.

15. What causes pinholes in a dope finish?

Excessive atomizing air pressure on the spray gun.

16. Why should the first coat of dope be thinned?

To ensure thorough penetration and encapsulation of all of the fibers.

17. Why is aluminum pigmented dope used on a fabric-covered aircraft?

To protect the clear dope and the fabric from the harmful effects of the sun.

18. What safety precaution must be observed when sweeping a paint room that has dried dope or lacquer overspray on the floor?

The floor must be wet down with water before it is swept. Static electricity from dry sweeping can cause a fire

19. Why should a fabric-covered surface be electrically grounded when dry-sanding it?

Dry-sanding can create enough static electricity on the surface that it can cause a spark and ignite the dope fumes inside the structure.

Typical Practical Projects

1. Mix dope and the correct thinner to get the proper viscosity for spraying. Demonstrate to the examiner the correct way to spray the dope on an aircraft surface.

2. Determine whether the dope on a piece of fabric-covered structure is nitrate or butyrate.

3. Demonstrate to the examiner the correct way of applying the first coat of dope to the fabric that is being installed on an aircraft structure.

4. Demonstrate to the examiner the correct way of dry sanding a fabric-covered aircraft wing.

5. Properly adjust the pressure of the air on a spray gun and pressure pot for spraying aircraft dope.

6. Explain to the examiner the reason for using aluminum-pigmented dope on a fabric-covered aircraft structure. Explain why it is important to not use too much aluminum dope.

7. Examine a defective dope finish and explain to the examiner the reason it is defective.

8. Apply aircraft dope using a brush on a fabric surface.

C. Task: Apply Finishes to STC'd Covering Materials

Reference: AMT-STRUC, Chapter 3

Typical Oral Questions

1. **What instructions must be followed when covering and finishing an aircraft with materials specified in a Supplemental Type Certificate (STC)?**
   The instructions that are a part of the STC.

2. **What finishing materials must be used when recovering an aircraft using an STC?**
   The finishing materials specified by the STC.

Typical Practical Projects

1. Using a copy of instructions for covering an aircraft structure supplied with an STC, explain to the examiner the way the aircraft should be covered.

2. Examine an aircraft that has been covered according to an STC, and explain to the examiner the way this differs from the factory-applied covering.

D. Task: Apply Paint Finishing Materials

Reference: AMT-STRUC, Chapter 3

Typical Oral Questions

1. **How thick should a coat of wash primer be that is used on an aluminum alloy aircraft structure?**
   It should be thin enough that it does not hide the surface of the metal.

2. **When mixing epoxy paint, should the converter be added to the resin or the resin to the converter?**
   The converter should always be added to the resin, never the resin to the converter.

3. **What are three types of primer that may be used when painting an aircraft?**
   Zinc chromate primer, wash primer, and epoxy primer.

4. **What type of thinner is used with zinc chromate primer?**
   Toluol or toluene.

5. What type of primer is used when the maximum protection of the metal is required?

Epoxy primer.

6. What should be done to a corroded aluminum alloy surface after the corrosion has been removed by mechanical methods?

The surface should be treated with a chemical conversion coating before the topcoats are applied.

7. What may be done to the surface to prevent filiform corrosion beneath the topcoat?

Be sure that the primer is properly and completely cured.

8. How is the finish removed from a fiberglass aircraft component that is being repaired?

The finish must be sanded off. Paint remover can soften the resin of which the component is made.

9. How can a vinyl film decal be removed from an aluminum alloy surface?

Place a cloth saturated with cyclohexanone or MEK over the decal until it is softened, and scrape it off of the surface with a plastic scraper.

Typical Practical Projects

1. Demonstrate to the examiner the correct way to spray a surface with a polyurethane enamel.

2. Identify the correct thinner to use with a list of finishing materials furnished by the examiner.

3. Properly adjust the pressure of the air on a spray gun and pressure pot for spraying aircraft dope.

4. Properly clean a piece of aluminum alloy and apply the correct amount of primer for best adherence of the topcoat material.

5. Properly remove the finish from a piece of fiberglass-reinforced aircraft structure so the structure can be repaired.

6. Properly prepare a composite or metallic structure for painting and identify all treatment and coating materials required.

7. Determine if a refinished control surface requires balancing.

Continued

Typical Practical Projects *Continued*

8. Indentify multiple types of aircraft finishes.

9. Inspect an acrylic nitrocellulose lacquer finish and describe your findings to the examiner.

E. Task: Inspect Finishes and Identify Defects

Reference: AMT-STRUC, Chapter 3

Typical Oral Questions

1. **What is a cause of poor adhesion between the topcoat and the fill coats on a fabric surface?**
   Too much aluminum powder in the aluminum pigmented dope.

2. **What is a cause of a rough finish on a freshly sprayed surface?**
   Too high atomizing air pressure on the spray gun.

3. **What causes sags and runs on a surface that has just been sprayed?**
   Too much finishing material being applied in one coat.

4. **What causes orange peel, or spray mottle, in a finish?**
   Incorrect paint viscosity or improper setting of the spray gun.

5. **What causes pinholes in a finish?**
   Excessive atomizing air on the spray gun.

6. **What causes blushing in a dope finish?**
   Too high humidity.

7. **What causes fisheyes in the finish?**
   Localized surface contamination.

Typical Practical Project

1. Inspect a painted surface for defects. Identify the type(s) of defects and explain to the examiner the proper corrective action.

IV. Area of Operation: Sheet Metal and Non-Metallic Structures
A. Task: Layout and Form a U-Channel or L-Angle

References: AMT-STRUC, Chapter 2; AC 43.13-1B, Chapter 4

Typical Oral Questions

1. **For maximum strength of a formed sheet metal fitting, should the bend be made along or across the grain of the metal?**
   Across the grain.

2. **What determines the minimum bend radius that can be used when forming a sheet metal structural fitting?**
   The alloy, the metal thickness, and its hardness.

3. **What is meant by the neutral axis in a sheet of metal?**
   A plane within the metal that neither stretches nor shrinks when the metal is being bent.

4. **What is a mold line in the development of a flat pattern for a formed metal part?**
   An extension of the flat sides beyond the radius.

5. **What is the bend tangent line?**
   A line in a flat pattern layout at which the bend starts.

6. **What is meant by setback?**
   The distance the jaws of a brake must be set back from the mold line to form a bend.

7. **What is meant by bend allowance?**
   The actual amount of metal in a bend. It is the distance between the bend tangent lines in a flat pattern layout.

8. **What is a sight line?**
   A line drawn on a flat pattern layout within the bend allowance that is one bend radius from the bend tangent line. When the sight line is directly below the nose of the radius bar on the brake, the bend will start at the bend tangent line.

9. **What type of device is a Cleco fastener?**
   A patented fastener that is inserted in the rivet holes and used to hold two pieces of sheet metal together until they can be riveted.

10. **What is the main function of throatless shears in an aircraft sheet metal shop?**
    Throatless shears are used to cut mild carbon steel up to 10-gage, and stainless steel up to 12-gage. They can be used to cut irregular curves in the metal.

11. **What kind of metal forming is done by a slip roll former?**
   Simple curves with a large radius.

12. **What kind of metal forming is done by bumping?**
   Compound curves in sheet metal.

13. **When forming a curved angle, what must be done to the flanges?**
   The flanges must be stretched for a convex curve and shrunk for a concave curve.

14. **When hand-forming a piece of sheet metal that has a concave curve, should the forming be started in the center of the curve, or at its edges?**
   Start at the edges and work toward the center.

15. **What is meant by a joggle in a piece of sheet metal?**
   A joggle is a small offset near the edge of a piece of sheet metal that allows the sheet to overlap another piece of metal.

Typical Practical Project

1. Lay out and form a channel of specified dimensions from a piece of aluminum alloy sheet. Use the minimum bend radius allowed for the material.

B. Task: Rivet Sheet-Metal Joints

References: AMT-STRUC, Chapter 2; AC 43.13-1B, Chapter 4

Typical Oral Questions

1. **What is the minimum edge distance allowed when installing rivets in a piece of aircraft sheet metal structure?**
   Two times the diameter of the rivet shank.

2. **What is the recommended transverse pitch to use when making a riveted two row splice in a piece of sheet metal?**
   Three-fourths of the distance between the rivets in the rows.

3. **Why should aluminum alloy rivets be driven with as few blows as is practical?**
   Excessive hammering will work-harden the rivets and make them difficult to drive.

4. **What determines whether a piece of sheet metal should be dimpled or countersunk when installing flush rivets?**
   The thickness of the sheet. Countersinking should be done only when the thickness of the sheet is greater than the thickness of the rivet head.

---

5. **What type of metal should be hot-dimpled?**

7075-T6, 2024-T81 aluminum alloys, and magnesium alloys should be hot-dimpled.

6. **What should be done to protect a riveted joint between aluminum alloy and magnesium alloy from corrosion?**

Coat the faying surface with a corrosion-inhibiting primer, dip the rivets in the primer and drive them while the primer is wet.

7. **Which stringer attached to a wing skin would require the greatest number of rivets for a splice?**

A stringer in the lower surface.

8. **What type of rivet may be used to replace a round head rivet in an aircraft structure?**

A universal head rivet.

9. **How long should a rivet be to join two pieces of sheet metal?**

The combined thickness of the metal sheets plus 1-1/2 times the rivet shank diameter.

10. **Should a riveted joint fail in shear or in bearing?**

It should fail in shear. The rivets should shear before the sheet tears at the rivet holes.

11. **What is the purpose of the beehive spring on a rivet gun?**

It holds the rivet set in the gun and allows the gun to vibrate the set.

Typical Practical Projects

1. Select the correct length and diameter of rivets furnished by the examiner, and properly install them to join two pieces of aluminum alloy sheet.

2. Given an assortment of aircraft rivets, identify each by their proper part number and the type of material.

3. Demonstrate to the examiner the correct way to set up and use a squeeze riveter.

4. Properly remove a series of rivets from a piece of aircraft structure.

5. Given a piece of metal with some improperly driven rivets in it, identify the cause of the bad rivets.

6. Lay out a rivet pattern for a circular patch of a size specified by the examiner.

7. Prepare and install a metal patch to repair damage.

Continued

---

8. Trim and form sheet metal to fit into a prepared area.

9. Install different types of special fasteners into a metallic structure.

10. Countersink holes in sheet metal assigned by the examiner with a .010" tolerance.

C. Task: Inspect and Test a Composite Structure

References: AMT-STRUC, Chapter 3; AC 43.13-1B, Chapter 3

Typical Oral Questions

1. **How can water entrapped in a honeycomb structure be detected?**
   By the use of radiographic inspection.

2. **What effect can entrapped moisture have on metal honeycomb structure?**
   Entrapped water can cause corrosion.

3. **What is the simplest way to detect delamination in a composite structure?**
   Tap the surface with the edge of a coin. If the material is sound, the tapping will result in a clear ringing sound; but if it is delaminated, the sound will be a dull thud.

4. **What type of nondestructive inspection is suitable for detecting internal damage in honeycomb material?**
   Ultrasonic inspection.

Typical Practical Projects

1. Demonstrate to the examiner the correct way to inspect a piece of composite material for delamination.

2. Demonstrate to the examiner the way to evaluate the surface condition of composite structure.

3. Explain to the examiner the correct way to use ultrasonic testing equipment to check the integrity of composite structure.

4. Inspect a composite material structure.

D. Task: Repair of Composite Structures

References: AMT-STRUC, Chapter 3; AC 43.13-1B, Chapter 3

Typical Oral Questions

1. **What kind of repair can be made to a small damage of the core material and one face sheet of a piece of aluminum alloy honeycomb structure?**
   A potted compound repair.

2. **What special precautions must be taken when repairing a radome?**
   Nothing must be done to the radome that will affect its electrical transparency or its aerodynamic strength

3. **How do you grind the point of a twist drill that is to be used for drilling transparent acrylic material?**
   The cutting edge should be dubbed off to a zero rake angle, and the included angle of the tip should be ground to 140 degrees.

4. **What is a warp clock in a structural repair manual?**
   An alignment indicator to show the orientation of the plies of a composite material. The ply direction is shown in relation to a reference direction.

5. **What are two advantages of laminated construction over riveted sheet metal?**
   Light weight and rigidity.

6. **What are two popular types of core material used in laminated structure?**
   Foam and honeycomb.

7. **What are two popular types of matrix material used in laminated structure?**
   Polyester and epoxy resins.

8. **What are the two parts of a polyester matrix material?**
   Resin and catalyst.

9. **What are the two parts of an epoxy matrix material?**
   Resin and hardener.

10. **What are the two types of resins used in aircraft construction?**
    Thermoplastic and thermosetting.

11. **What is necessary to cure a thermosetting resin?**
    Heat.

12. What are three materials that may be used to reinforce the matrix material for aircraft structure?

Fiberglass, Kevlar®, and graphite.

13. What is meant by a unidirectional fabric?

A fabric in which all of the major fibers run in the same direction.

14. What is meant by the ribbon direction of a honeycomb material?

The direction in a piece of honeycomb material that is parallel to the length of the strips of material that make up the core.

15. What are two types of repair to a damaged honeycomb core composite material?

Room-temperature cure repair and hot-bond repair.

16. What is meant by the shelf life of a material?

The normal length of time a material can be expected to keep its usable characteristics if it is stored and not used.

17. What is meant by the pot life of a resin?

The length of time a resin will remain workable after the catalyst has been added.

18. What document lists the safety hazards associated with a resin used in composite structure?

The Material Safety Data Sheet for that resin.

Typical Practical Projects

1. Repair a small damage to a piece of honeycomb structure.

2. Demonstrate to the examiner the correct way to check a bonded honeycomb structure for indication of internal delamination.

3. Using a Material Safety Data Sheet, explain to the examiner the proper procedure to use if a person in your shop gets some of the material in his or her eye.

4. Install special fasteners into a composite structure.

E. Task: Inspect and Repair Transparent Plastic Windows

References: AMT-STRUC, Chapter 3; AC 43.13-1B, Chapter 3

Typical Oral Questions

1. **Of what class of resins are aircraft windows and windshields made?**
   Thermoplastic.

2. **What type of transparent plastic material is used for most aircraft windshields?**
   Acrylic plastic.

3. **How should sheets of transparent plastic material be stored?**
   Leave the protective paper on the material and store it tilted approximately 10° from the vertical.

4. **How tight should the screws be tightened when installing an acrylic windshield in a channel?**
   Tighten the screw to a firm fit and back it off one full turn.

5. **What is meant by crazing of a transparent plastic material?**
   Tiny hair-like cracks that may not extend all of the way to the surface. Crazing is caused by stresses or chemical fumes.

6. **What type of material is used to remove surface damage to a piece of acrylic resin?**
   Micro-Mesh® abrasive sheets.

Typical Practical Projects

1. Demonstrate the correct way to clean an acrylic plastic windshield.

2. Demonstrate the correct way to remove minor scratches from the surface of a piece of acrylic plastic material.

3. Demonstrate the correct way to repair a crack in an aircraft side window.

4. Inspect acrylic windshields.

5. Identify window enclosure materials.

V. Area of Operation: Welding
A. Task: Gas Welding

References: AMT-STRUC, Chapter 2; AC 43.13-1B, Chapter 4

Typical Oral Questions

1. **What are the two fuel gases most generally used for gas welding?**
   Oxygen and acetylene.

2. **What fuel gases are used for welding aluminum?**
   Oxygen and hydrogen.

3. **What are two types of torches used in gas welding?**
   Balanced-pressure torches and injector torches.

4. **What color lenses are used for gas welding steel?**
   Green or brown.

5. **What color lenses are used for gas welding aluminum?**
   Blue.

6. **Why is it important that the pressure of the gas in an acetylene cylinder be kept low?**
   Acetylene gas becomes unstable when it is kept under pressure of more than about 15 psi.

7. **What determines the amount of heat that is put into a weld by an oxy-acetylene torch?**
   The size of the orifice in the torch tip.

8. **What is the difference in the appearance of an oxidizing flame, a neutral flame, and a reducing flame produced by an oxy-acetylene torch?**
   An oxidizing flame has a pointed inner cone, and the torch makes a hissing noise. A neutral flame has a rounded inner cone, and there is no feather around the inner cone. A reducing flame has a definite feather around the inner cone.

9. **What is one method of minimizing distortion when making a long butt weld?**
   Skip welding minimizes distortion. Tack weld the materials together and then complete the welds between the tacks, starting at a tack and working back toward the finished weld.

10. **What is meant by tack welding?**
    Tack welding is the use of small welded spots to hold the material together until the final bead is run.

11. **Why must thick plates of metal be preheated before they are welded?**

    Preheating is a method of controlling the expansion and contraction of the metal being welded. Preheating minimizes the stresses that are caused when welding thick metal.

12. **What must be done to an aircraft structure after it has been welded while clamped in a heavy jig or fixture?**

    It must be normalized by heating it to a uniform red heat and allowed to cool slowly in still air.

13. **Why is it important that all traces of the welding flux be removed after a piece of aluminum or magnesium is welded?**

    Welding flux is corrosive and it must be removed to keep the metal from corroding.

14. **What is the difference between brazing and welding?**

    In brazing, the base metal is not melted, but is covered with a low-melting-point alloy. In welding, the base metal is melted.

15. **What kind of flame should be used when gas welding aluminum?**

    A soft, neutral oxy-hydrogen flame.

16. **What is an acceptable acetylene line pressure to use when welding with an oxy-acetylene rig?**

    About 5 psi.

17. **What kind of flame should be used when gas welding stainless steel?**

    A slightly carburizing flame.

18. **How much should the bead penetrate the material when welding two pieces of steel with a butt weld?**

    The joint should have 100% penetration.

19. **What is meant by a soft flame?**

    A soft flame is one that is made when the pressures of the gases are low enough that the flame does not make a noise and does not blow the puddle.

20. **What must be done to an aircraft fuel tank before it can be repaired by welding?**

    The gasoline fumes must all be purged from the tank by running live steam through it for at least 30 minutes, by soaking it in hot water, or by filling it with nitrogen or carbon dioxide.

Typical Practical Projects

1. Demonstrate the correct way to set up oxy-acetylene welding equipment.

2. Demonstrate the correct way to light the torch and adjust it to get a neutral flame.

3. Demonstrate the correct way to shut down oxy-acetylene welding equipment.

4. Given an example of a bad weld, identify the cause of the problem and explain to the examiner the way it should have been welded.

5. Select the correct welding rods for a specified welding method.

6. Fabricate a silver solder joint.

7. Braze a lap joint.

8. Fabricate a butt weld using oxy-acetylene.

B. Task: Gas Tungsten Arc Welding (GTAW)

Reference: AMT-STRUC, Chapter 2

Typical Oral Questions

1. **What is another name for GTA welding?**
   TIG welding.

2. **What type of shielding gases are used for GTA welding?**
   Helium and argon.

3. **Why is GTA welding preferred over oxy-acetylene welding for building and repairing welded steel tube aircraft structure?**
   The heat is concentrated in the weld and does not cause as much distortion as gas welding.

4. **What is the function of the inert gas used in GTA and GMA welding?**
   The inert gas forms a shield to keep oxygen away from the weld puddle so oxides cannot form and weaken the weld.

5. **What is used as the electrode in GTA welding?**
   A small-diameter tungsten wire.

6. What are three types of power that can be used for GTA welding?

DC-straight polarity, DC-reverse polarity, and AC.

7. Which type of power provides the greatest heat and deepest penetration in GTA welding?

DC-straight polarity.

8. Which type of power is used for GTA welding aluminum and magnesium?

DC-reverse polarity.

Typical Practical Projects

1. Correctly set up a GTA welding rig, and make a proper bead across a piece of steel.

2. Evaluate a weld specified by the examiner, noting the penetration, size and smoothness of the weld bead, and the distance from the weld that the metal was heated.

3. Locate the cleaning methods for magnesium prior to welding.

4. Fabricate a diamond weld patch.

C. Task: Fabricate Tubular Structures

References: AMT-STRUC, Chapter 2; AC 43.13-1B, Chapter 4

Typical Oral Questions

1. What type of repair can be used when a steel structural tube is dented to more than 1/4 of its circumference?

A patch may be welded over the damage.

2. What type of repair can be used when a steel structural tube is dented at a cluster?

A patch may be welded over the damaged area with fingers extending up along each member of the cluster.

3. What is the preferred method of splicing a new piece of tubing into a structure?

An inner sleeve splice.

4. How is the inner sleeve tube held in the structural tube until the gap is welded?

It is held in place with rosette welds.

---

5. What is one limitation of using an outer-sleeve splice in an aircraft structure?
This type of splice is not suitable where it would cause a bulge in the fabric.

6. How should the ends of an outer-sleeve be cut?
Cut it with a 30° fishmouth.

Typical Practical Projects

1. Prepare two pieces of steel tubing, and weld them together to form a T.

2. Evaluate a cluster weld specified by the examiner to determine if it is airworthy, and if not, why.

3. Determine the repair procedure for a defect in a tubular structure.

D. Task: Soft Solder Wire and Connector

Reference: AMT-STRUC, Chapter 2

Typical Oral Questions

1. What is the function of the flux used in soldering?
Flux covers the cleaned and heated metal to keep oxygen away from it so oxides cannot form. Oxides keep the solder from adhering to the surface of the metal.

2. What kind of solder is recommended for soldering electrical wires?
60/40 resin-core solder.

3. What is the composition of 60/40 solder?
60% tin and 40% lead.

4. What is the difference between soldering and brazing?
Soldering is a method of joining metal parts with a molten nonferrous alloy that melts at a temperature below 800°F. Brazing is essentially the same except the brazing alloy melts at a temperature higher than 800°F but lower than the melting temperature of the metal on which it is used.

5. Why must acid-core solder never be used on electrical wire?
The acid causes the wire to corrode.

6. What determines the strength of a soldered joint?
The mechanical connection of the joint, not the solder.

Typical Practical Projects

1. Demonstrate to the examiner the correct way to make a soft-solder connection between two stranded copper wires.

2. Demonstrate to the examiner the correct way to solder a stranded copper wire into a quick-disconnect connector.

VI. Area of Operation: Assembly and Rigging

A. Task: Install a Control Surface

Reference: AMT-STRUC, Chapter 4

Typical Oral Questions

1. What is the function of the ailerons on an airplane?

Ailerons rotate the airplane about its longitudinal axis.

2. What is a stabilator?

A single-piece horizontal tail surface that acts as both the horizontal stabilizer and the elevators. A stabilator pivots about its front spar.

3. What is the function of the elevators on an airplane?

Elevators rotate the airplane about its lateral axis.

4. What is the function of the rudder on an airplane?

The rudder rotates the airplane about its vertical axis.

5. What is the purpose of an aileron balance cable?

It ties the ailerons together in such a way that when one aileron deflects downward the other one is pulled upward.

6. What is an aerodynamically balanced control surface?

A surface with part of its area ahead of the hinge line. When the surface is deflected, the portion ahead of the hinge aids the movement.

7. What is meant by differential aileron travel?

Aileron movement in which the upward-moving aileron deflects a greater distance than the one moving downward. The up aileron produces parasite drag to counteract the induced drag produced by the down aileron.

8. **What is a Frise aileron?**

An aileron with its hinge line set back from the leading edge so that when it is deflected upward, part of the leading edge projects below the wing and produces parasite drag to help overcome adverse yaw.

9. **What is a ruddervator?**

Movable control surfaces on a V-tail airplane that are controlled by both the rudder pedals and the control yoke. When the yoke is moved in or out, the ruddervators move together and act as the elevators. When the rudder pedals are depressed, the ruddervators move differentially and act as a rudder.

10. **How much is a fairlead allowed to deflect a control cable?**

No more than 3°.

11. **Why are the control cables of large airplanes normally equipped with automatic tension regulators?**

The large amount of aluminum in the aircraft structure contracts so much as its temperature drops in flight that the control cables could become dangerously loose. The automatic tension regulators keep the cable tension constant as the dimensions of the aircraft change.

12. **In what publication could you find correct control surface movement for a particular airplane?**

In the Type Certificate Data Sheet for the airplane.

Typical Practical Projects

1. Install a control surface on an airplane specified by the examiner. Rig the cables to the proper tension and adjust the stops so the surface will have the correct travel as specified in the TCDS. Properly safety the turnbuckles.

2. Properly install a swaged control cable terminal or a Nicopress sleeve type terminal. Explain the way to check the terminal for proper installation.

3. Check the flight controls of an airplane, including all of the secondary controls for the correct direction of movement when the cockpit controls are moved.

4. Demonstrate to the examiner the correct way to inspect a piece of aircraft control cable for indication of internal corrosion.

5. Locate leveling methods.

6. Locate flight control neutral positions.

7. Verify the alignment of an empennage or landing gear.

Continued

---

8. Inspect a primary and secondary control surface assigned by the examiner.

9. Assemble aircraft components.

10. Remove and reinstall a primary flight control cable.

11. Adjust a push-pull control system.

B. Task: Rig Rotary Wing Aircraft

Reference: AMT STRUC, Chapter 4

Typical Oral Questions

1. **What causes dissymmetry of lift produced by the rotor of a helicopter?**

   The forward speed of the helicopter produces dissymmetry of lift. The rotor blade that is traveling forward as the helicopter is flying produces more lift than the blade that is traveling rearward.

2. **Why do single-rotor helicopters use an auxiliary rotor on their tail?**

   The thrust from the tail rotor counteracts the torque produced by the main rotor.

3. **Why is it important that the blades of a helicopter rotor system be in track?**

   If the blades are not in track, vertical vibration can develop.

4. **What is the function of the collective pitch control of a helicopter?**

   It changes the pitch of all the blades at the same time. The collective pitch controls the vertical flight of the helicopter.

5. **What is the function of the cyclic pitch control?**

   It changes the pitch of the rotor blades at a particular point in their rotation to tilt the plane of the rotor. The cyclic pitch controls the lateral movement of the helicopter.

6. **What is the function of the tail rotor on a single main rotor helicopter?**

   The thrust from the tail rotor counteracts the torque of the main rotor to control the yaw of the helicopter. The control pedals change the pitch of the tail rotor blades to vary the thrust.

7. **What is the purpose of the stabilizer system in a helicopter?**

   A helicopter is statically stable but dynamically unstable. The stabilizer system restores the helicopter to level flight when outside forces cause it to pitch or roll.

8. **What is meant by a fully articulated rotor system?**

   It is a rotor system in which the individual blades are free to flap, drag, and feather.

9. **What is meant by a semirigid rotor system?**

   A two-blade rotor system in which the blades can feather, but cannot flap nor drag. The rotor hub is mounted on the mast with a teetering hinge that allows the entire rotor to rock as a unit.

10. **What is meant by a rigid rotor system?**

    A rotor system that has freedom of motion about its feather axis only. The flexibility of the blades is sufficient to provide the needed flapping and dragging.

11. **What is the basic cause of low-frequency lateral vibration?**

    The main rotor blades being out of static balance.

12. **What is the basic cause of low-frequency vertical vibration?**

    One of the main rotor blades producing more lift than the other.

13. **What is usually the cause of high frequency vibration?**

    The engine, cooling fan, or tail rotor.

14. **What is the most effective way to check a helicopter rotor for dynamic balance?**

    Use a special computerized analyzer/balancer.

Typical Practical Projects

1. Demonstrate to the examiner the correct way to check a helicopter rotor for track.

2. Demonstrate to the examiner the way to check the control rods for proper installation and safetying.

3. Explain to the examiner the operation of the swashplate of a helicopter rotor system.

4. Locate the causes of vertical vibration in a two rotor helicopter rotor system.

C. Task: Balance Flight Control Surfaces

Reference: AMT-STRUC, Chapter 4

Typical Oral Questions

1. **Why is it important that control surfaces be statically balanced?**

   An out-of-balance control surface can cause severe flutter.

2. Where can you find the specifications for balancing the control surfaces of an airplane?

In the aircraft maintenance manual.

3. What in addition to static unbalance can cause a control surface to flutter?

Worn hinges or improperly adjusted control cable tension.

Typical Practical Project

1. Remove a control surface from an aircraft, check its static balance as instructed in the aircraft maintenance manual, and reinstall it. Check the condition of the hinges and rig the control cables for the proper tension.

D. Task: Jack Aircraft

Reference: AMT-STRUC, Chapter 4

Typical Oral Questions

1. Where can you find instructions for jacking one wheel of an aircraft to change a tire?

In the aircraft maintenance manual.

2. Where can you find instructions for jacking the complete aircraft to perform a landing gear retraction test?

In the aircraft maintenance manual.

3. Where can you find instructions for hoisting an aircraft to replace wheels with floats?

In the aircraft maintenance manual.

Typical Practical Project

1. Demonstrate to the examiner the correct way to position the jacks under the wing of an airplane to raise it off the hangar floor. Explain the safety procedures that must be observed.

VII. Area of Operation: Airframe Inspection

A. Task: Aircraft Inspections

References: AMT-SYS, Chapter 14; 14 CFR Parts 43 and 91

Typical Oral Questions

1. **What must the mechanic give the owner or operator of an aircraft if the aircraft he is giving a 100-hour inspection to proves to be unairworthy?**

   A signed and dated list of all of the discrepancies that keep the aircraft from being airworthy.

2. **Where can you find the recommended statement to use for recording the approval or disapproval of an aircraft for return to service after a 100-hour inspection?**

   In 14 CFR §43.11.

3. **Under what conditions can an aircraft be operated with a 100-hour inspection overdue?**

   The aircraft can be operated for no more than 10 hours after an inspection is due for the purpose of flying it to a place where the inspection can be performed.

4. **For how long can an aircraft be operated if a 100-hour inspection is overdue?**

   For no more than 10 hours. The time beyond the 100 hours must be subtracted from the time before the next inspection is due.

5. **Under what conditions can an aircraft that is due an annual inspection be operated?**

   It can only be flown when a special flight permit is issued.

6. **What certification is required for a mechanic to be able to approve an aircraft for return to service after a 100-hour inspection?**

   A mechanic certificate with Airframe and Powerplant ratings.

7. **What determines whether or not an aircraft must be given a 100-hour inspection?**

   Aircraft that carry persons for hire and aircraft that are used for flight instruction for hire must be given 100-hour inspections.

8. **What is the difference between an annual inspection and a 100-hour inspection?**

   The inspections themselves are identical. An annual inspection can be conducted only by an A&P mechanic who holds an Inspection Authorization, while a 100-hour inspection can be performed by an A&P mechanic without an IA.

9. **What certification is required for a mechanic to conduct an annual inspection and approve the aircraft for return to service after the inspection?**

    A mechanic certificate with Airframe and Powerplant ratings and an Inspection Authorization.

10. **What is a progressive inspection?**

    An inspection of the same level as an annual inspection but approved by the FAA to be performed on a schedule that does not require the aircraft to be out of service for the time necessary to perform the entire inspection all at once.

11. **Does the FAA require that a checklist be used when conducting an annual or a 100-hour inspection?**

    Yes, according to 14 CFR §43.15(c)(1).

12. **What certification is required for a mechanic to conduct a progressive inspection?**

    A mechanic certificate with an Airframe and Powerplant ratings and an Inspection Authorization.

13. **Where can you find the requirements for inspecting the altimeter and static systems of aircraft operated under Instrument Flight Rules?**

    In 14 CFR Part 43, Appendix E.

14. **Where can you find the requirements for inspecting the ATC transponder that is installed in an aircraft?**

    In 14 CFR Part 43, Appendix F.

15. **What items must be inspected on a helicopter in accordance with the instructions for Continued Airworthiness?**

    The drive shafts or similar systems, the main rotor transmission gear box, the main rotor and center section, the auxiliary rotor.

16. **Must all manufacturer's service letters, instructions, and bulletins be complied with on an annual or 100-hour inspection?**

    Not unless they have been incorporated into an airworthiness directive.

17. **For how long must the record of a 100-hour inspection be retained in the aircraft maintenance records?**

    For one year, or until the next 100-hour inspection is completed.

18. **For how long must the record of the current status of life-limited parts of an engine be retained?**

    This is part of the permanent records and it must be retained and transferred with the aircraft when it is sold.

Typical Practical Projects

1. Determine from the aircraft records furnished by the examiner whether or not any repetitive Airworthiness Directives must be complied with on a 100-hour inspection.

2. Using the aircraft model and serial number specified by the examiner, determine what Airworthiness Directives apply to the aircraft. Examine the aircraft maintenance records to determine if all of the applicable ADs have been complied with.

3. Determine from the aircraft records furnished by the examiner when the next 100-hour inspection is due, and when the next annual inspection is due.

4. Prepare an aircraft for a 100-hour inspection. Perform the inspection. Make the correct maintenance record entries to show that the inspection has been conducted.

5. Describe to the examiner the record entry that must be made when an altimeter system has been inspected in accordance with 14 CFR §91.411 and 14 CFR Part 43, Appendices E and F.

6. Perform a conformity inspection on an engine, propeller, or airframe assigned by the examiner.

Section 2 Airframe Systems and Components

I. Area of Operation: Aircraft Landing Gear Systems
A. Task: Inspect and Service Landing Gear

Reference: AMT-STRUC, Chapter 6

Typical Oral Questions

1. **Where may the instructions for greasing a retractable landing gear on an aircraft be found?**

   In the aircraft maintenance manual.

2. **Where may a list of the approved lubricants for greasing an aircraft retractable landing gear be found?**

   In the aircraft maintenance manual.

3. **Where can you find safety precautions for jacking an aircraft for retractable landing gear inspection and maintenance?**

   In the aircraft maintenance manual.

4. **What is the purpose of the centering cam in a nose-wheel shock strut?**

   The centering cam forces the nose wheel straight back with the strut before it is retracted into the nose-wheel well.

5. **How does a shimmy damper keep a nose wheel from shimmying?**

   It acts as a small hydraulic shock absorber between the piston and the cylinder of the nose-wheel shock strut.

Typical Practical Projects

1. Demonstrate to the examiner the correct way to jack an aircraft to perform a landing gear retraction test.

2. Demonstrate to the examiner the correct way to lubricate a retractable landing gear.

3. Explain to the examiner the way a particular retractable landing gear is prevented from retracting when the weight of the aircraft is on it.

4. Troubleshoot a retractable landing gear system.

5. Adjust the nose wheel steering.

Continued

---

6. Inspect the landing gear alignment.

7. Troubleshoot a nose wheel steering system.

B. Task: Service Landing Gear Shock Strut

Reference: AMT-STRUC, Chapter 6

Typical Oral Questions

1. **Where can you find the specifications for the type of fluid used to service an aircraft landing gear shock strut?**
   On the nameplate on the strut.

2. **What absorbs the initial landing impact in an oleo shock strut?**
   The transfer of oil from one compartment to another through a metered orifice.

3. **What absorbs the taxi shocks in an oleo shock strut?**
   The compressed air or nitrogen.

4. **How much oil should be put into an oleo shock strut?**
   With the strut completely deflated, fill it to the level of the filler plug.

5. **How much air or nitrogen should be put into an oleo shock strut?**
   With the strut serviced with fluid and the filler plug in place and the weight of the aircraft on the strut, put in enough air or nitrogen to extend the piston to the height specified in the aircraft maintenance manual.

6. **What is the purpose of using an exerciser jack when servicing a shock strut with fluid?**
   The jack moves the piston up and down inside the cylinder to work all of the air out of the oil to be sure that the proper amount of oil is in the strut.

Typical Practical Projects

1. Demonstrate to the examiner the correct way to service an oleo shock strut:
   — Select the correct fluid.
   — Explain the safety procedures to follow.
   — Put in the correct amount of fluid.
   — Put in the correct amount of air.

2. Inspect a nose-wheel shimmy damper, and service it with fluid if it is needed.

3. Check the main wheels of an aircraft for the proper amount of camber, and toe-in or toe-out.

4. Replace an air/oil shock strut air valve.

5. Troubleshoot an air/oil shock strut.

C. Task: Replace Brake Linings

Reference: AMT-STRUC, Chapter 6

Typical Oral Questions

1. **Where can you find a list of brake fluids approved for the aircraft?**
   In the aircraft service manual.

2. **What is used to flush brake lines and cylinders if the system uses vegetable-base fluid?**
   Alcohol.

3. **What is used to flush brake lines and cylinders if the system uses mineral-base fluid?**
   Naphtha, varsol, or Stoddard solvent.

4. **How do you measure the amount of brake lining wear on single disk brakes?**
   Measure the clearance between the disk and the inboard side of the brake housing with the brakes applied.

5. **What is the purpose of the debooster in a hydraulic power brake system?**
   The debooster decreases the pressure and increases the volume of fluid going to the brakes. This gives the pilot better control of the brakes.

6. **What should be done to hydraulic brakes when the pedal has a spongy feel?**
   The spongy feel is caused by air in the brake. The brakes should be bled of this air.

7. **What is the purpose of the compensator port in the master cylinder of aircraft brakes?**

   The compensator port in the master cylinder opens the brake reservoir to the wheel cylinders when the brakes are off. This prevents pressure from building up in the brake lines and causing the brakes to drag.

8. **What is the purpose of the shuttle valve in the brake system of an aircraft using hydraulic power brakes?**

   The shuttle valve is an automatic transfer valve. It allows the brakes to be operated by hydraulic system pressure under all normal conditions; but if this pressure is lost, it allows the brakes to be operated by the emergency backup system.

9. **How does an antiskid brake system keep the wheels of an aircraft from skidding on a wet runway?**

   The antiskid system monitors the rate of deceleration of the wheels. If any wheel slows down faster than it should (as it would at the beginning of a skid), the pressure on the brake in that wheel is released until the wheel stops decelerating, then the pressure is reapplied.

Typical Practical Projects

1. Demonstrate your ability to check brake-lining wear and the condition of the disk on an aircraft specified by the examiner, and replace the lining.

2. Demonstrate the correct way to bleed brakes on an aircraft specified by the examiner.

3. Demonstrate the correct way to check the fluid level in a brake master cylinder and determine the correct type of fluid.

4. Demonstrate the correct way to replace the seals in the wheel cylinder of a single-disk brake.

D. Task: Disassemble and Inspect a Landing Gear Wheel

Reference: AMT-STRUC, Chapter 6

Typical Oral Questions

1. **When removing a wheel from an aircraft to change the tire, when should the tire be deflated?**

   After the aircraft is on the jacks, but before the axle nut is loosened.

---

2. What should be used to deflate high-pressure tires?

A deflator cap screwed onto the tire valve, to allow the air to escape through the hole in the side of the cap and not in the face of the mechanic.

3. What is used in a split wheel to keep air from leaking between the two wheel halves?

An O-ring seal.

4. Where are cracks most likely to form in an aircraft wheel?

In the bead seat area.

5. What type of inspection should be used to inspect the bead seat area of a wheel for cracks?

Eddy current inspection.

Typical Practical Projects

1. Demonstrate to the examiner the correct way to jack one wheel of an aircraft, remove the wheel, disassemble the wheel, and remove the tire.

2. Demonstrate the correct way to inspect the wheel for cracks and corrosion.

3. Demonstrate the correct way to check and install the center O-ring, to mount the tire on the wheel, torque the wheel nuts, and inflate the tire.

4. Demonstrate the correct way to pack the wheel bearings with grease, install the wheel on the aircraft, adjust the axle nut, and safety it on the axle.

E. Task: Inspect and Service a Landing Gear Tire

Reference: AMT-STRUC, Chapter 6

Typical Oral Questions

1. What is meant by the ply rating of a tire?

The number of plies of cotton fabric needed to produce the same strength as the actual plies in the tire.

2. What is the function of the bead in a tire?

The bead is made of high-strength carbon steel wire bundles and used to provide the strength and stiffness where the tire mounts on the wheel.

3. Is it proper to use a tube in a tubeless tire?

No, the inner liner of a tubeless tire is rough and it can chafe the tube in normal operation.

---

4. **What is the function of the grooves cut into the tread of a tire?**

   The grooves produce the optimum traction with the runway surface.

5. **What is the most widely used tread pattern for modern airplane tires?**

   A series of straight grooves around the periphery of the tire.

6. **How should new aircraft tires be stored?**

   In a dark, cool location away from electrical motors or battery chargers.

7. **Is it best to store new tires vertically or horizontally?**

   Vertically.

8. **What is the most important maintenance procedure for aircraft tires?**

   Keep them properly inflated.

9. **What should be used to remove oil from a tire?**

   Mild soap and warm water.

10. **Where do you find the proper inflation pressure for an aircraft tire?**

    In the aircraft service manual.

11. **Why should aircraft tire pressure be rechecked after it has been installed for about 24 hours with no load applied?**

    The tire will stretch and the pressure will drop. The proper pressure must be restored.

12. **What causes an aircraft tire to wear more on the shoulders than in the center of the tread?**

    Operating the tire in an underinflated condition.

13. **What causes an aircraft tire to wear more in the center of the tread than on the shoulders?**

    Operating the tire in an overinflated condition.

14. **What should be done to an aircraft tire if the sidewalls are weather-checked enough to expose the cord?**

    The tire should be scrapped.

15. **Why is it important that some aircraft with retractable landing gear be given a retraction test after new or retreaded tires are installed?**

    It is possible in some aircraft that a new or retreaded tire can be different enough in size from the previous tire that it could lock up in the wheel well when the landing gear is retracted.

16. **What safety procedure should be followed when inflating a tire on a large aircraft wheel for the first time after it as been replaced?**

Put the wheel in a safety cage when it is being inflated because of the danger if the through bolts should fail.

17. **What should be done with a tire that was on a wheel which was overheated enough to melt the fusible plug in the wheel?**

The tire should be scrapped.

18. **Where can you find the correct inflation pressure for the tires on an aircraft?**

In the aircraft service manual.

Typical Practical Projects

1. Demount a tire from an aircraft wheel, inspect the tire for wear, explain to the examiner the conditions that could cause a tire to be unairworthy.

2. Install a tire on a wheel and inflate it to the proper pressure. Explain to the examiner the safety procedures to follow.

3. Repair a defective tire tube.

4. Replace a tire or tube valve core and check for leaks.

5. Locate tire storage practices.

II. Area of Operation: Hydraulic and Pneumatic Power Systems
A. Task: Remove, Clean and Install Hydraulic Filter

Reference: AMT-STRUC, Chapter 5

Typical Oral Questions

1. **What kind of filter is a micronic filter?**

A filter with a special paper element.

2. **What is a double-action pump?**

A pump that delivers fluid with the movement of the pump handle in both directions.

3. **Why do most engine-driven hydraulic pumps have a shear section in their drive couplings?**

If the pump should seize, the shear section will break, disconnecting the pump from the engine and preventing further damage.

---

4. **What does an unloading valve do in a hydraulic system?**

   The unloading valve, or pressure regulator, controls system pressure by shifting the pump outlet fluid from the pressurized system back into the reservoir when the system pressure is high enough. The fluid circulates with very little load on the pump until the system pressure drops to the regulator kick-in value. The pump then forces fluid into the system until the pressure builds back up to the regulator kick-out value.

5. **What is the purpose of an accumulator in an aircraft hydraulic system?**

   The accumulator holds pressure on the hydraulic fluid in the system. The pressure is held by compressed air or nitrogen acting on the fluid through a bladder, a diaphragm, or a piston.

6. **What is the purpose of an orifice check valve in an aircraft hydraulic system?**

   An orifice check valve allows full flow of fluid in one direction through the valve, but restricts the flow in the opposite direction.

7. **Where are line-disconnect fittings normally located in an aircraft hydraulic system?**

   Normally in the lines that connect the engine-driven pump to the aircraft hydraulic system.

8. **What is a single-action hydraulic actuating cylinder?**

   A linear actuating cylinder that uses hydraulic fluid under pressure to move the piston in only one direction. The piston is returned by a spring.

9. **What is a sintered metal hydraulic filter?**

   A surface filter whose element is made of powdered metal fused under heat and pressure.

10. **What is the purpose of the differential pressure indicator on a hydraulic filter?**

    It indicates when the filter is clogged and fluid is bypassing the filter element.

11. **What is a Cuno filter?**

    An edge filter made of a stack of thin metal disks separated by thin scraper blades. Contaminants collect on the edge of the disks and are periodically scraped out by rotating the disks. The contaminants collect in the bottom of the filter case for future removal.

Typical Practical Projects

1. Inspect a hydraulic system filter and service it according to the instructions of the aircraft manufacturer.

2. Check the contaminants in a hydraulic filter and explain to the examiner the probable source of the contaminants and what action, if any, should be taken.

B. Task: Remove and Install a Hydraulic Seal

Reference: AMT-STRUC, Chapter 5

Typical Oral Questions

1. **Is a chevron seal a one-way or a two-way seal?**
   A one-way seal.

2. **To which side of a chevron seal should the pressure be applied?**
   To the open side.

3. **Is an O-ring seal a one-way or a two-way seal?**
   A two-way seal.

4. **How can you be sure of getting an O-ring made of the correct material for a specific hydraulic component?**
   The O-ring must have the correct part number and it must have been obtained from a reputable source.

5. **On which side of an O-ring should the backup ring be placed?**
   On the side away from the source of pressure.

6. **What should be done to the sharp edges of threads and actuator pistons when installing O-rings?**
   The sharp edges should be covered with paper.

Typical Practical Project

1. Demonstrate the correct way to select and install an O-ring seal in a hydraulic actuator.

C. Task: Inspect and Service a Pneumatic Power System

Reference: AMT-STRUC, Chapter 5

Typical Oral Questions

1. **What are two basic differences between a hydraulic and a pneumatic system?**
   The fluid in a pneumatic system is compressible and that used in a hydraulic system is incompressible. A pneumatic system has no return system.

2. **What are two functions of a low-pressure pneumatic system in an aircraft?**
   To operate the gyros in flight instruments, and to inflate pneumatic deicer boots.

---

3. **What type of pump is used in a low-pressure pneumatic system?**

    A vane-type pump.

4. **Why do high-altitude aircraft that have pneumatic gyro instruments use pressure-actuated instruments rather than vacuum-actuated instruments?**

    At high altitude there is not enough air mass to drive the gyros at their required speed.

5. **What effect would a dirty inline air filter have on the operation of pneumatic gyro instruments?**

    The instruments would not get enough air to spin up to their required speed.

6. **Of what material are the vanes in a dry type air pump made?**

    Carbon.

7. **What kind of device is used to control the speed of movement of the piston in a pneumatic actuator?**

    A variable orifice.

8. **What is the purpose of the moisture separator in a high-pressure pneumatic system?**

    The separator collects moisture from the air and holds it on a baffle until the system is shut down. When the inlet pressure to the moisture separator drops below 450 psi, a drain valve opens and all of the accumulated moisture is discharged overboard. A moisture separator removes about 98% of the moisture in the air.

9. **What are two types of filters that are used in an aircraft pneumatic system?**

    Micronic (paper) type, and screen type.

Typical Practical Projects

1. Demonstrate to the examiner the correct way to install a filter in a low-pressure pneumatic system.

2. Service the emergency air bottle in an aircraft brake system with the correct amount of air or nitrogen.

3. Troubleshoot a pneumatic power system leak.

4. Adjust a pneumatic power system relief valve.

D. Task: Service a Hydraulic Reservoir

Reference: AMT-STRUC, Chapter 5

Typical Oral Questions

1. **What are the two basic types of hydraulic fluid used in modern aircraft?**
   Mineral base fluid and phosphate ester base fluid.

2. **Does the main hydraulic pump take its fluid from the bottom of the reservoir, or from a standpipe?**
   The main pump normally takes its fluid from a standpipe, while the emergency pump takes its fluid from the bottom of the reservoir. If a break in the system should allow the main pump to pump all of its fluid overboard, there will still be enough fluid in the reservoir to allow the emergency system to extend the landing gear and actuate the brakes.

3. **Why are some hydraulic reservoirs pressurized?**
   Pressurization ensures that fluid will be supplied to the inlet of the pumps at high altitude where there is not enough atmospheric pressure to do this.

4. **What are two ways aircraft hydraulic reservoirs may be pressurized?**
   By an aspirator in the fluid return line or by bleed air from one of the engine compressors.

5. **What is used to flush a hydraulic system that uses Skydrol hydraulic fluid?**
   Trichlorethylene or the solvent recommended by the aircraft manufacturer.

6. **What is used to flush a hydraulic system that uses mineral base hydraulic fluid?**
   Naphtha, varsol or Stoddard solvent.

7. **Where can you find the type of hydraulic fluid required for a particular aircraft?**
   In the maintenance manual for the aircraft. This information is also on a placard on the system reservoir.

8. **What is used to remove phosphate-ester base hydraulic fluid from aircraft tires?**
   Soap and water.

9. **How can you be sure that a replacement seal in a hydraulic component is compatible with the fluid used in the system?**
   Use only the seal identified by part number that is specified in the component maintenance manual.

10. **What must be done to the lines that are disconnected when replacing an aircraft hydraulic system component?**
   They must be capped with the correct fluid line cap or plug. Masking tape or other types of adhesive tape should never be used.

11. What must be done before a pressurized reservoir is serviced?

All of the pressure must be bled off.

Typical Practical Projects

1. Demonstrate to the examiner the correct way to service a pressurized hydraulic reservoir.

2. Determine the correct type of hydraulic fluid required by a particular aircraft and check the system for the correct amount of fluid.

3. Service a hydraulic accumulator.

4. Purge air from a hydraulic system.

E. Task: Inspect and Service Hydraulic Pumps and Valves

Reference: AMT-STRUC, Chapter 5

Typical Oral Questions

1. **Explain the difference between a single-acting and double-acting hand pump.**

   Single-action pumps move fluid on only one direction of handle operation. Double-acting hand pumps move fluid on both directions of handle movement.

2. **What type of pump is a gear pump considered?**

   A gear pump is a constant displacement, high pressure pump.

3. **What type of pump is a piston pump with a variable cam plate considered?**

   Fuel pumps may be divided into two distinct system categories: (1) constant displacement and (2) variable displacement. A piston pump with a variable cam changes the effective (not actual) length of each piston stroke. This makes this type of pump a variable displacement with constant pressure.

4. **What is the difference in function between a pressure regulator and a pressure relief valve?**

   Pressure regulators control overall system pressure. Pressure relief valves act a back-up to the pressure regulator to prevent overpressure damage to the system and components.

5. **If a system requires a lower pressure than system pressure, what type of valve is used?**

   A pressure reducer valve.

Typical Practical Projects

1. Remove and install a hydraulic selector valve.

2. Check a pressure regulator for performance and adjust as necessary.

3. Remove, install, and check an engine-driven hydraulic pump.

4. Troubleshoot a hydraulic power system.

5. Remove and/or install a system pressure relief valve.

6. Troubleshoot hydraulic power system leaks.

III. Area of Operation: Cabin Atmosphere Control Systems

A. Task: Inspecting and Testing an Exhaust Heating System

Reference: AMT-SYS, Chapter 9

Typical Oral Questions

1. **Where does the warm air come from that is used to heat the cabin of most small single-engine reciprocating-engine-powered aircraft?**
   From a shroud around the engine muffler.

2. **What is the danger of a leak in an exhaust system cabin heater?**
   Exhaust gases contain carbon monoxide (CO), a colorless, odorless, gas that can cause incapacitation or death to the aircraft occupants.

3. **How can an exhaust system be checked for leaks?**
   Pressurize it with the discharge from a vacuum cleaner and wipe the outside of the system with a soap solution. Any leak will cause bubbles to form.

4. **How can you tell that there is carbon monoxide in the aircraft cabin?**
   Indicator crystals in a CO detector will change color, from a normally bright color to a dark color. At lethal levels of CO they will turn black.

Typical Practical Project

1. Inspect for leaks in the portion of the engine exhaust system that supplies heat for the aircraft cabin heater.

B. Task: Inspect and Operate a Combustion Heater System

Reference: AMT-SYS, Chapter 9

Typical Oral Questions

1. **Where does the fuel used in an aircraft combustion heater come from?**

   From the aircraft fuel tanks.

2. **What happens to a combustion heater if the flow of ventilating air is restricted?**

   If the ventilating air is restricted and the temperature reaches a preset value, the limit switch will cause the fuel to be shut off to the heater.

3. **What regulates the temperature in an aircraft cabin that is heated with a combustion heater?**

   A thermostat senses the cabin temperature and cycles the fuel valve on or off to maintain the temperature at the desired value.

4. **What maintenance is required for a combustion heater?**

   Clean the fuel filters and check for fuel leaks.

Typical Practical Project

1. Inspect a combustion heater in an aircraft; explain to the examiner the way the system operates, and the precautions that should be taken in its operation.

C. Task: Inspect and Operate of a Vapor-Cycle Cooling System

Reference: AMT-SYS, Chapter 9

Typical Oral Questions

1. **What are two types of air conditioning systems that may be installed on an aircraft?**

   Air-cycle systems and vapor-cycle systems.

2. **How is the heat removed from an aircraft cabin with a vapor-cycle air conditioning system?**

   The cabin heat is absorbed by the refrigerant in the evaporator, then carried outside the aircraft where it is given up to the outside air in the condenser.

3. **What produces the cool air in a vapor-cycle air conditioning system?**

    Warm cabin air is blown across the evaporator, where its heat is transferred into the refrigerant. The air that leaves the evaporator is cool.

4. **What is used as the refrigerant in a vapor-cycle air conditioning system?**

    A Freon-type liquid refrigerant known as Refrigerant 12, or the more environmentally friendly R-134a.

5. **What is the state of the refrigerant as it leaves the compressor?**

    It is a high-pressure gas.

6. **What is the state of the refrigerant as it leaves the condenser?**

    It is a high-pressure liquid.

7. **What is the state of the refrigerant as it leaves the thermostatic expansion valve?**

    It is a low-pressure liquid.

8. **What is the state of the refrigerant as it leaves the evaporator?**

    It is a low-pressure vapor.

9. **How is the compressor lubricated?**

    Refrigeration oil is mixed with the refrigerant and it circulates through the compressor and the entire system.

10. **What is the function of the thermostatic expansion valve?**

    It meters just enough liquid refrigerant into the evaporator that all of it will be evaporated by the time it leaves the evaporator coils.

11. **How is refrigerant put into the system?**

    It is put into the system through service valves on the low side of the system using a manifold gage set.

12. **How should the components in the low side of a properly operating vapor-cycle cooling system feel?**

    They should feel cool.

13. **How is a vapor-cycle cooling system checked for refrigerant leaks?**

    Hold the probe of an electronic leak detector below any suspect fitting or component. If there is a leak, the tone of the sound produced by the detector will change.

14. **What safety equipment should be worn when charging a vapor-cycle cooling system?**

    A safety face shield that protects the entire face.

Typical Practical Projects

1. Given a schematic diagram of a vapor-cycle cooling system, explain the function of each of the components to the examiner.

2. Demonstrate to the examiner the correct way to add refrigerant to a vapor-cycle cooling system.

3. Demonstrate to the examiner the correct way to check a vapor-cycle cooling system for refrigerant leaks.

4. Locate the sources of contamination in a Freon system.

5. Locate the operating instructions for a Freon system.

D. Task: Inspect and Operate an Air-Cycle Cooling System

Reference: AMT-SYS, Chapter 9

Typical Oral Questions

1. **Where does the warm air come from that is used to heat the cabin of a large jet transport aircraft?**

   Warm engine compressor bleed air is used.

2. **Where is the first place the hot compressor bleed air gives up some of its heat in an air-cycle cooling system?**

   In the primary heat exchanger.

3. **What is the function of the air-cycle machine in an air-cycle cooling system?**

   The centrifugal compressor increases the pressure and temperature of the bleed air. This high temperature air gives up some of its heat in the secondary heat exchanger, and a great deal more as it drives the expansion turbine. It leaves the expansion turbine as cold air.

4. **Why must air-cycle air conditioning systems incorporate a water separator?**

   The rapid cooling of the air in the expansion turbine causes moisture to condense in the form of fog. This moisture is trapped in the moisture separator before the air is released into the cabin.

5. **How is the temperature of the air produced by an air-cycle cooling system controlled?**

   By a temperature control valve which mixes hot engine compressor bleed air with cold air from the expansion turbine.

E. Task: Inspect and Operate a Cabin Pressurization System

Reference: AMT-SYS, Chapter 9

Typical Oral Questions

1. **Why are the cabins of most turbine-powered aircraft pressurized?**
   These aircraft fly at such high altitudes that supplemental oxygen would be needed for the occupants if the cabins were not pressurized.

2. **Where does the pressurizing air come from on most turbine-powered aircraft?**
   From air bled from one of the engine compressors.

3. **Where does the pressurizing air come from on most smaller reciprocating-engine-powered aircraft?**
   From the engine turbocharger.

4. **What determines the amount of pressurization that an aircraft can use?**
   The structural strength of the aircraft cabin.

5. **How is cabin pressure controlled in a pressurized aircraft?**
   More pressure than is needed is pumped into the aircraft cabin, and the pressure controller modulates the outflow valve to maintain the correct pressure in the cabin.

6. **What is meant by the isobaric mode of cabin pressurization?**
   The isobaric mode of cabin pressurization is the mode that keeps the cabin altitude constant as the aircraft changes its flight altitude.

7. **What is meant by the constant differential mode of cabin pressurization?**
   After the pressure in the aircraft cabin reaches the maximum value allowed by structural considerations, the constant differential mode of operation holds the pressure inside the cabin a constant amount above the outside air pressure.

8. **What is the function of the cabin outflow valve on a pressurized aircraft?**
   The cabin outflow valve, which is controlled by the pressure controller, maintains the correct amount of pressure inside the cabin.

9. **What is the function of the cabin pressure safety valve on a pressurized aircraft?**

   The cabin pressure safety valve prevents cabin pressure from exceeding the maximum allowable differential pressure.

10. **Why must pressurized aircraft have a negative pressure relief valve?**

    The structure of an aircraft cabin is not designed to tolerate the inside pressure being lower than the outside pressure.

11. **What keeps the cabin of a pressurized aircraft from being pressurized when the aircraft is on the ground?**

    A squat switch on the landing gear holds the safety valve open when the aircraft is on the ground.

Typical Practical Projects

1. Given a schematic diagram of an aircraft pressurization system, explain to the examiner the function of each of the components.

2. On a pressurized aircraft specified by the examiner, locate and identify the source of pressurizing air, the cabin outflow valve, the cabin pressure safety valve, and the cabin pressure controller.

3. Locate the instructions for the inspection of a pressurization system.

F. Task: Leak Test Gaseous Oxygen System

Reference: AMT-SYS, Chapter 9

Typical Oral Questions

1. **What are the two main gases that make up our atmosphere?**
   Nitrogen and oxygen.

2. **What is used to check an oxygen system for leaks?**
   A special leak-detector liquid that is a form of non-oily soap.

3. **Why must fittings in an oxygen system not be tightened to stop a leak when there is pressure on the system?**
   When the system is pressurized the tubing is expanded slightly; if the fitting is tightened when it is expanded, it will likely leak when the pressure is reduced.

4. What are three ways supplemental oxygen can be carried in an aircraft?

As a high-pressure gas, in its liquid form, and as a solid in the form of a chemical candle.

5. What kind of gaseous oxygen must be used to service an aircraft oxygen system?

Only aviators' breathing oxygen. Hospital oxygen and welding oxygen contain too much moisture to be used.

6. What is a continuous-flow oxygen system?

An oxygen system that continuously flows a metered amount of oxygen into the mask.

7. What is a pressure-demand oxygen system?

An oxygen system that flows oxygen to the mask only when the wearer of the mask inhales. Above a specified altitude, the regulator meters oxygen under pressure into the mask when the wearer inhales.

8. What identification must be stamped on an oxygen bottle carried in an aircraft?

The identification DOT 3AA or DOT 3HT, the date of manufacture, and the date of all of the hydrostatic tests.

9. To what pressure, and how often should DOT 3AA oxygen cylinders be hydrostatically tested?

They should be tested to 5/3 of their working pressure every three years.

10. To what pressure, and how often should DOT 3HT oxygen cylinders be hydrostatically tested, and when should they be retired from service?

They should be tested to 3,083 psi every three years and retired from service after 15 years or 4,380 pressurizations, whichever occurs first.

Typical Practical Projects

1. Demonstrate to the examiner the correct way to check an oxygen system for leaks.

2. Demonstrate to the examiner the correct way to service an installed oxygen system.

G. Task: Replace an Oxygen Valve or Fitting

Reference: AMT-SYS, Chapter 9

Typical Oral Questions

1. **What kind of lubricant can be used for installing fittings in an oxygen system component?**
   Teflon tape or a special water-base lubricant.

2. **What is used to check for leaks after replacing a fitting in an oxygen system?**
   A special leak-detector liquid that is a form of non-oily soap.

3. **What cleaning solutions can be used to clean parts used in an oxygen system?**
   Anhydrous ethyl alcohol, isopropyl alcohol, or freon.

4. **What may be used to dry components in an oxygen system after they have been cleaned?**
   Water-pumped dry nitrogen.

5. **What may be used to purge the lines in an oxygen system after it has been opened for servicing?**
   Water-pumped dry nitrogen.

6. **What must be done before any maintenance can be done on an oxygen system?**
   The oxygen supply must be turned off at the bottle valve.

Typical Practical Projects

1. Check the oxygen bottles in an aircraft for the required identification marks and for the status of their hydrostatic tests.

2. Demonstrate to the examiner the correct way to remove and install a oxygen valve or fitting.

3. Demonstrate to the examiner the correct way to purge an oxygen system to remove all traces of air from the lines.

4. Demonstrate to the examiner the correct way to service an oxygen system with the proper type and amount of oxygen.

5. Demonstrate to the examiner the correct way to check an oxygen system for leaks.

IV. Area of Operation: Aircraft Instrument Systems
A. Task: Swing a Magnetic Compass

Reference: AMT-SYS, Chapter 10

Typical Oral Questions

1. **What error is corrected when an aircraft compass is swung?**
   Deviation error.

2. **What fluid is used in an aircraft magnetic compass?**
   A special water-clear fluid similar to kerosine.

3. **What is the maximum amount of deviation error allowed when a magnetic compass is installed in an aircraft?**
   10 degrees.

4. **Where on an airport is a compass rose located?**
   At a location where there is little traffic and the area is free from magnetic interference caused by electrical power lines or buried pipes.

5. **What is done to a compass to correct for deviation error?**
   The compensating magnets in the compass are adjusted to minimize the effect of outside magnetic fields.

6. **Where should the compass correction card be placed?**
   In plain sight of the pilot, near the compass.

Typical Practical Project

1. Demonstrate to the examiner the correct way to swing a compass and record the results.

2. Locate the instructions for the inspection of a magnetic compass.

B. Task: Replace Vacuum or Pressure System Filter

Reference: AMT-SYS, Chapter 10

Typical Oral Questions

1. **What are the gyroscopic instruments that are connected to the low-pressure pneumatic system of an aircraft?**
   Heading indicator, attitude indicator, and turn-and-slip indicator.

2. **What device is used with a wet-pump vacuum system to prevent oil from getting into the deicer boots?**

An oil separator.

3. **What are two types of filters used with a pressure system for gyros?**

A pump inlet filter and an inline filter.

4. **What type of filter is used with a vacuum system for gyros?**

A central air filter.

Typical Practical Project

1. Demonstrate the correct way to change the filter in the gyro instrument system of an aircraft specified by the examiner.

C. Task: Replace Vacuum or Pressure System Pump

Reference: AMT-SYS, Chapter 10

Typical Oral Questions

1. **What two types of pumps are used in the low-pressure pneumatic system?**

A dry-type and a wet-type air pump.

2. **What are the vanes of a wet-type air pump made of?**

Steel.

3. **What are the vanes of a dry-type air pump made of?**

Carbon.

4. **How are the vanes of a wet-type air pump lubricated?**

With engine oil directed into the pump through a small hole in the base of the pump.

5. **Why is it important to use the correct gasket when replacing a wet-type air pump?**

The gasket must have a hole through which the pump lubricating oil can flow.

6. **Why do dry-type air pumps not need to be lubricated?**

The special carbon material of which the vanes are made wears away in microscopic amounts to provide the needed lubrication.

---

7. What must be done to the gyro pressure system if a dry-type air pump fails?

All of the filters must be replaced to prevent any debris from the pump vanes getting into the gyro instruments.

Typical Practical Project

1. Identify an aircraft vacuum system.

2. Demonstrate the correct way to change the air pump in the low-pressure pneumatic system of an aircraft specified by the examiner.

3. Adjust the gyro/instrument air pressure.

D. Task: Install a Sensitive Altimeter

Reference: AMT-SYS, Chapter 10

Typical Oral Questions

1. Who is authorized to perform the altimeter tests to determine the accuracy of the altimeter?

The manufacturer of the aircraft on which the tests are conducted, or a certificated repair station properly equipped and authorized to perform the test.

2. Where are the requirements for the altimeter system tests found?

14 CFR Part 43, Appendix E.

3. How often should an altimeter be checked if it is installed in an aircraft used in IFR flight?

Every 24 calendar months.

4. What are 6 tests that must be made when testing an altimeter?

Scale error, hysteresis, after-effect, friction, case leak, and barometric scale error.

5. How much difference is allowed between the altitude indication on the automatic pressure altitude reporting equipment and that on the altimeter?

125 feet.

6. To what altitude must altimeters be tested?

To the highest altitude the aircraft will be flown on IFR flight.

---

7. What record must be made of a test of an altimeter?

The aircraft permanent maintenance record must show the date, the maximum altitude to which the altimeter was tested, and the name of the person approving the aircraft for return to service after the test.

8. Do the tests described in 14 CFR Part 43, Appendix E apply to the altimeters installed in all certificated aircraft?

No, only those operated under instrument flight rules in controlled airspace.

9. To what avionic equipment is the output from an encoding altimeter connected?

The ATC transponder.

10. What is the allowable difference between the surveyed elevation of the airport and the indication on the altimeter when it is set to the local altimeter setting?

75 feet.

Typical Practical Project

1. Demonstrate the correct way to install a sensitive altimeter, and check the indication of the altimeter when the barometric scale is set to the local altimeter setting.

E. Task: Perform Static System Check

Reference: AMT-SYS, Chapter 10

Typical Oral Questions

1. What instruments in an aircraft are connected to the static system?

The airspeed indicator, vertical speed indicator, and altimeter.

2. Who is authorized to conduct a static system tests specified in 14 CFR §91.411?

A certificated mechanic holding an airframe rating.

3. How much leakage is allowed in the static system of an unpressurized aircraft?

With a pressure differential of 1 inch of mercury, the system must not show a loss of indicated altitude of more than 100 feet in one minute.

4. How much leakage is allowed in the static system of a pressurized aircraft?

With a pressure differential equal to the maximum cabin differential pressure for which the aircraft is certificated, the system must not show a loss of indicated altitude of more than 2 percent of the equivalent altitude of the maximum cabin differential pressure or 100 feet, whichever is the greater, in one minute.

---

5. **What indication on the altimeter shows that the pressure inside the static system has been decreased by 1 inch of mercury?**

   The altimeter will show an increase of approximately 1,000 feet.

6. **When should a static system leak check be performed?**

   Any time the static system has been opened.

7. **What should be done to the static port that is not being used to conduct the leak test?**

   It should be taped over in such a way that the tape can not be overlooked or forgotten when the test is completed.

Typical Practical Projects

1. Perform a static system check on an aircraft specified by the examiner. Determine from the proper source if the system meets the requirements for flight under Instrument Flight Rules.

2. Check the pitot heater to determine whether or not it is functioning properly.

3. Remove and install a heated pitot tube.

4. Locate the alternate air source on an aircraft.

F. Task: Check Instrument Systems

Reference: AMT-SYS, Chapter 10.

Typical Oral Questions

1. **What is are the differences between absolute, gauge, and differential pressure instrument systems?**

   An absolute pressure instrument, such as an altimeter, measures actual pressure. Gauge pressure instruments measure the difference between exiting barometric pressure and pressure inside a sealed container such as a Bourdon tube or a bellows. Differential pressure instruments display the difference between two pressures, such as pitot pressure and static pressure used to display airspeed.

2. **Why is the length of a thermocouple lead important?**

   Thermocouple accuracy is dependent on the resistance of the circuit. Lead lengths are designed for specific installations and should never be altered.

3. **A failure of an airspeed indicator needle to move is likely caused by what problem?**

   A blockage in the pitot head will prevent the creation of a differential pressure.

---

4. **Explain the difference between variation and deviation in a compass system.**

   Compass variation is caused by the difference between the earth's magnetic and geographic poles. Aeronautical charts display magnetic variation. Compass deviation is caused by all other magnetic fields aside from the earth's magnetic and geographic poles. Deviation may be caused by magnetic fields in the aircraft.

5. **What may be causing an attitude indicator to not properly erect or display?**

   Gyroscopes are dependent on achieving and maintaining proper rotational speed. Failure to do so may be caused by low vacuum created by the vacuum system or motor failure in an electrically-driven gyroscope.

6. **What do the green, yellow, and red arc markings on instrument mean?**

   Green indicates normal operating range, yellow indicates caution operating range, and red indicates prohibited operating range.

7. **Can an A&P technician repair an instrument with a cracked glass?**

   No. The instrument must be replaced.

Typical Practical Projects

1. Remove and install instruments.

2. Install range markings on instrument glass.

3. Check for proper operation of a manifold pressure gauge.

4. Apply instrument glass slippage marks.

5. Locate procedure for troubleshooting vacuum operated turn-and-bank instruments.

6. Identify an electric attitude indicator.

7. Locate a servo-type indicating system.

8. Identify the exhaust gas temperature system components.

9. Explain how to troubleshoot an electrical resistance thermometer system.

10. Inspect a cylinder head temperature indicating system.

11. Locate and explain the troubleshooting procedures for a directional gyro system malfunction.

V. Area of Operation: Communications and Navigation Systems
A. Task: Replace ELT Batteries

Reference: AMT-SYS, Chapter 11

Typical Oral Questions

1. **On what two frequencies does the Emergency Locator Transmitter operate?**
   121.5 and 243.0 megahertz.

2. **Where is the ELT transmitter normally located on an aircraft?**
   In the tail of the aircraft or as far aft as possible, so it will be least likely to be damaged in a crash.

3. **How often should ELT batteries be replaced or recharged?**
   When the transmitter has been in use for more than 1 cumulative hour, or when 50% of their useful life or charge has expired.

4. **How can you know when an ELT battery must be replaced or recharged?**
   By the date marked on the outside of the transmitter.

5. **How often must ELTs be inspected for proper installation, battery corrosion, operation of the controls and sensor, and the presence of the radiated signal?**
   Every 12 calendar months.

6. **What causes an ELT to actuate?**
   An inertia switch that detects an impact parallel to the longitudinal axis of the aircraft as would occur in a crash.

7. **How is an ELT tested to determine that it is working?**
   Actuate the test switch and listen on 121.5 or 243.0 MHz. Make the test during the first five minutes of the hour and do not allow the ELT to operate for more than 3 sweeps. If the ELT is operated outside of this time frame, you should contact the control tower before conducting the test.

Typical Practical Projects

1. Demonstrates to the examiner the correct way to check the status of the ELT batteries, and to replace or recharge them as is appropriate.

2. Demonstrate to the examiner the way to determine that the ELT is not transmitting when the aircraft is being shut down.

3. Demonstrate to the examiner the correct way to check the ELT for operation.

B. Task: Check, Install, and Troubleshoot a Coaxial Cable with BNC Connectors

Reference: AMT-SYS, Chapter 11

Typical Oral Questions

1. **What kind of conductor is used to connect a VHF or UHF antenna to the receiver or transmitter?**
   Coaxial cable.

2. **What is a coaxial cable?**
   A type of two-conductor electrical cable in which the center conductor is encased in insulation inside a braided shield that serves as the outer conductor. Coaxial cables are normally used for attaching radio receivers and transmitters to antennas.

3. **How can you determine the proper coaxial cable and connectors to use in an aircraft radio installation?**
   Refer to the radio installation instructions for the correct part number for the cable and connectors.

4. **What precautions should be taken when installing coaxial cable between a radio transmitter and its antenna?**
   The routing should be as direct as possible, there should be no sharp bends in the coax, and it should be kept away from heat that could soften the insulation.

5. **What is a BNC connector?**
   A coaxial cable connector that is connected by inserting the guide pins on the male connector into slots in the female connector and twisting the connector one quarter turn.

Typical Practical Project

1. Correctly install a BNC connector on a piece of coaxial cable.

2. Inspect a coaxial cable for security.

C. Task: Identification of Antennas

Reference: AMT-SYS, Chapter 11

Typical Oral Questions

1. **What is the preferred location for a VOR antenna on an airplane?**
   On top of the aircraft, along the center line of the fuselage.

---

2. Which component of the Instrument Landing System shares the antenna with the VOR?

The ILS localizer.

3. What is the preferred location for a DME antenna?

Along the center line of the belly of the aircraft, as far from any other antenna as is practical.

4. What kind of antenna is used for VHF communications?

A vertically polarized whip antenna.

5. What kind of antenna is used for the ATC transponder?

A UHF slub antenna.

6. What is the preferred location for the ATC transponder antenna?

On the center line of the belly of the aircraft as far from any other antenna as is practical.

7. What two types of antenna are used with most ADF receivers?

A directional loop antenna and a nondirectional sense antenna.

8. Why is it necessary to install a doubler on the inside of the aircraft skin when antenna is mounted on the skin?

The doubler reinforces the skin so wind loads on the antenna will not cause the skin to flex and crack.

Typical Practical Project

1. Locate and identify the antenna for the VOR, the DME, the ATC transponder, the ADF, and the glide slope, and the VHF communications equipment.

2. Identify the transponder transmission line.

3. Locate the installation procedures for antennas including mounting and coaxial connections.

D. Task: Check Autopilot for Proper Operation

Reference: AMT-SYS, Chapter 11

Typical Oral Questions

1. **What is the basic purpose of an autopilot?**
   It frees the human pilot from continuously having to fly the aircraft, and flies with a high degree of precision. It also couples with various electronic navigational aids.

2. **What are the basic subsystems of an automatic flight control system?**
   Command, error-sensing, correction, and follow-up.

3. **What type of device is normally used in the error-sensing subsystem?**
   Gyros.

4. **What are three types of servos that are used in the correction subsystem?**
   Hydraulic, pneumatic, and electric.

5. **What is the purpose of the follow-up subsystem in an autopilot?**
   It stops the control movement when the surface has deflected the proper amount for the signal sent by the error sensor.

Typical Practical Projects

1. Demonstrate to the examiner the correct way to check the proper operation of an autopilot.

2. Locate and identify to the examiner the servos used in an autopilot system.

E. Task: Install a Nav/Com Radio

Reference: AMT-SYS, Chapter 11

Typical Oral Questions

1. **Is a certificated airframe mechanic allowed to adjust a communications transmitter?**
   No, this requires a license issued by the Federal Communications Commission.

2. **Which frequency band is used for most aircraft communications?**
   The VHF band, between 30 and 300 megahertz.

3. In which frequency band does the VOR equipment operate?

In the VHF band, between 108.0 and 117.95 megahertz.

4. In what frequency band does the DME equipment operate?

In the UHF band, between 962 and 1,024 megahertz, and between 1,151 and 1,213 megahertz.

5. Which frequency band is used for long-range communications from an aircraft?

The high frequency band (2 to 25 megahertz).

6. What is meant by a transceiver?

It is a piece of radio communications equipment in which all of the circuits for the receiver and the transmitter are contained in one housing.

Typical Practical Projects

1. Demonstrate to the examiner the correct way to install and check the operation of a VHF nav/com transceiver.

2. Make the proper entry in the aircraft records for the installation of the transceiver. Include the revised weight and balance record.

3. Inspect the electronic equipment mounting base for security and condition.

4. Inspect the electronic equipment shock-mounting bonding jumpers for security and resistance.

5. Inspect the static discharge wick for security and resistance.

6. Make a required list of placards for communication and navigation equipment.

VI. Area of Operation: Aircraft Fuel Systems

A. Task: Inspect, Service, and Replace Fuel System Transmitters

Reference: AMT-SYS, Chapter 8

Typical Oral Questions

1. What is used as the sensor in the fuel tank for an electronic-type fuel quantity indicating system?

Tubular capacitors that extend across the fuel tank from top to bottom.

---

2. **What is the principle upon which the electronic-type fuel quantity indicating system operates?**

   Tubular capacitors extending across the fuel tanks change their capacitance as the fuel level changes. The dielectric constant (k) of the fuel is approximately twice that of air.

3. **What is used as a sensor in the fuel tank for the older resistance-type fuel quantity indicating system?**

   A variable resistor with an arm that is moved by a float riding on top of the fuel in the tank.

4. **What are two types of fuel cells used in modern aircraft?**

   Integral fuel cells (cells that are a sealed-off portion of the structure), and bladder-type cells.

5. **Why are fuel tanks divided into compartments or have baffles installed in them?**

   The compartments or baffles keep the fuel from surging back and forth as the aircraft changes its attitude in flight.

6. **What is the purpose of a drip gage in the fuel tank of a large aircraft?**

   The drip gage allows a mechanic to check the fuel level in a tank from the bottom of the tank.

7. **What markings must appear near the filler opening of the fuel tanks on reciprocating-engine-powered aircraft, and on a turbine-powered aircraft?**

   On a reciprocating engine powered-aircraft: the word "Avgas" and the minimum grade of fuel.

   On a turbine engine powered aircraft: the words "Jet Fuel," the permissible fuel designations, the maximum permissible fueling supply pressure, and the maximum permissible defueling pressure.

8. **Where can you find the correct part number for the fuel quantity sensor to be installed in an aircraft fuel tank?**

   In the Illustrated Parts Catalog for the aircraft.

9. **When must the fuel quantity indicating system indicate "zero?"**

   During level flight when the fuel in the tank is equal to the unusable fuel supply.

Typical Practical Projects

1. Demonstrate to the examiner the way to perform the following operations on an electronic-type fuel quantity indicating system:
    a. Locate the correct part number for the fuel tank probe specified by the examiner.
    b. Install the probe in the fuel tank.
    c. Calibrate the system in accordance with instructions given by the aircraft manufacturer.
    d. Make the appropriate maintenance record for the replacement of the fuel tank probe.

2. Demonstrate to the examiner the correct way to use a fuel drip gage to measure fuel quantity.

3. Inspect a remote fuel indicating system.

4. Locate the fuel system's operating instructions.

5. Locate the fuel system's inspection instructions

6. Locate the fuel system's defueling procedures.

7. Troubleshoot the fuel pressure warning system.

8. Locate the troubleshooting procedures for fuel temperature systems.

9. Remove and/or install a fuel quantity transmitter.

10. Troubleshoot fuel systems.

B. Task: Service a Fuel System Strainer

Reference: AMT-SYS, Chapter 8

Typical Oral Questions

1. **Where are fuel system strainers located?**
   One strainer is located in the outlet to the tank, and the main strainer is located in the fuel line between the outlet of the fuel tank and the inlet to the fuel metering device.

2. **Why do the fuel strainer used on some turbine-engine aircraft have a warning device that signals the flight crew when the strainer is beginning to clog up?**
   Strainers clog because ice forms on the filter element. The flight crew can route the fuel through a fuel heater to melt the ice.

3. **What must be done after a fuel system strainer has been cleaned or replaced?**

   The system must be tested for leaks by pressurizing the system with the boost pump, if one is used.

Typical Practical Project

1. Demonstrate to the examiner the way to perform the following operations on the main fuel strainer of the aircraft specified by the examiner:
   a. Remove and properly clean the strainer element.
   b. Reinstall the strainer element and check the filter for leaks.
   c. Safety the strainer by the method specified by the aircraft manufacturer.

2. Locate the fuel system inspection instructions.

3. Troubleshoot the fuel system.

C. Task: Drain Fuel Sumps

Reference: AMT-SYS, Chapter 8

Typical Oral Questions

1. **Why is it important to drain all of the fuel sumps before the first flight of the day?**

   Water can condense in the fuel tanks and it must be drained out before the aircraft is safe for flight.

2. **Is the procedure of draining the sumps with the aircraft in the ground attitude an assurance that all of the water is removed from the tanks?**

   No, some aircraft require special procedures to remove all of the water. Refer to the Aircraft Flight Manual or Pilot's Operating Handbook.

3. **How does water appear in the fuel drained from the tank sumps?**

   Water appears as a clear globlule in the bottom of the container used to collect the fuel drained from the sumps.

4. **What color is grade 100-LL fuel?**

   Blue.

5. **How can you detect jet fuel in the sample taken from the tank sump drains?**

   Jet fuel is basically clear and it has an odor similar to kerosine.

---

6. What must be done if the sump drains sample shows traces of jet fuel?

The fuel system must be drained and flushed out with the proper grade of aviation gasoline.

Typical Practical Projects

1. Locate in the proper documentation the correct grade of fuel to be used in an aircraft specified by the examiner.

2. Demonstrate to the examiner the correct way to sample the fuel taken from tank sump drains. Explain the way to detect water and rust contamination, and contamination with jet fuel.

D. Task: Remove and Install a Fuel Tank Valve

Reference: AMT-SYS, Chapter 8

Typical Oral Questions

1. **Why must an aircraft fuel valve have a detent in its operating mechanism?**

   The detent gives the pilot a positive indication by feel when the selector valve is in the full ON and full OFF position.

2. **What must be done before a fuel selector valve can be removed from an aircraft?**

   The tank to which the valve is connected must be drained or otherwise isolated.

3. **What must be done after a fuel valve is replaced?**

   The fuel system must be checked for leaks.

4. **How is a fuel leak indicated on a reciprocating-engine-powered aircraft?**

   The dye in the gasoline stains the area around the leak.

E. Task: Inspect Fuel Tanks

Reference: AMT-SYS, Chapter 8

Typical Oral Questions

1. What is the function of the sump in a fuel tank?

The sump, or lowest point, in a fuel tank is located below the fuel outlet. The sump collects water and contaminants and will have a drain to remove them.

2. What are the three different types of fuel tanks?

Built-up tanks, integral tanks, and bladder tanks.

3. What problem can occur in a bladder tank with a blocked vent?

As internal tank pressure decreases, the pressure differential between the atmosphere and the tank can cause the tank restraints to fail and the tank can collapse and block the fuel outlet.

4. How do you prepare an aluminum fuel tank for welding?

Remove all fuel and thoroughly wash the tank, inside and out, with hot water and detergent. The tank should be purged with live steam for at least 30 minutes to remove all residual fuel and vapors.

5. After welding an aluminum fuel tank, what pressure should the tank be tested with?

3.5 psi.

Typical Practical Projects

    1. Inspect a metal fuel tank.

    2. Inspect a bladder fuel tank.

    3. Inspect an integral fuel tank.

VII. Area of Operation: Aircraft Electrical Systems

A. Task: Replace an Electrical Switch

Reference: AMT-SYS, Chapter 7

Typical Oral Questions

1. Why must a switch be derated if it is used in a circuit that supplies incandescent lamps?

The high-inrush current caused by the low resistance of the cold filaments requires that the switches be derated.

2. What is an SPDT switch?

A single-pole, double-throw switch.

3. Where could you find the part number of a switch in an aircraft electrical system?

In the equipment table or bill of materials on the electrical circuit diagram for the aircraft.

4. If no specific instructions are available, which way should the operating handle of an electrical switch move to turn a component on?

Forward or upward.

Typical Practical Project

    1. Select the proper switch to replace one specified by the examiner, install it, check its operation, and record the replacement in the aircraft maintenance records.

    2. Based on a given electrical circuit, select and install the appropriate switches.

B. Task: Replace a Circuit Breaker

Reference: AMT-SYS, Chapter 7

Typical Oral Questions

1. **What is meant by a trip-free circuit breaker?**

   A circuit breaker that cannot be closed while a fault exists, regardless of the position of the operating handle.

2. **What is meant by a slow-blow fuse?**

   A fuse that will allow more current than its rating to flow for a short period of time, but will open the circuit if more than its rated current continues to flow.

3. **What is the function of a fuse or circuit breaker in an aircraft electrical circuit?**

   It protects the wiring from an excess of current. It will open the circuit if enough current flows to heat the wire until the insulation begins to smoke.

4. **What are two principles upon which circuit breakers operate?**

   Magnetic circuit breakers open a circuit when the current creates a strong enough magnetic field. Thermal circuit breakers open a circuit when the current causes enough heat.

5. **What circuit in an aircraft electrical system is not required to have a circuit protective device?**

   The main circuit for starter motors, used during starting only.

6. **Is an automatic-reset circuit breaker approved for aircraft electrical circuits?**

   No, a manual operation is needed to restore service after the circuit breaker has tripped.

Typical Practical Project

1. Select the proper circuit breaker to replace one specified by the examiner, install it, check its operation and record the replacement in the aircraft maintenance records.

2. Based on a given electrical system, select and install fuses and/or circuit breakers.

C. Task: Splice and Install Electrical Wire

Reference: AMT-SYS, Chapter 7

Typical Oral Questions

1. **What two things must you take into consideration when selecting the wire size to use in an aircraft electrical system installation?**

   The current carrying capability of the wire and the voltage drop caused by the current flowing through the wire.

2. **What is the maximum number of wires that should be connected to any single stud in a terminal strip?**

   Four.

3. **How is a wire bundle protected from chafing where the bundle goes through a hole in a fuselage frame or bulkhead?**

   The edges of the hole are covered with a flexible grommet, and the bundle is secured to the structure with a cushioned clamp.

4. **What kind of clamp is used to secure a wire bundle to the aircraft structure?**

   A cushioned clamp.

5. **Why are solderless splices usually better than soldered splices in the wiring of an aircraft electrical system?**

   Soldered joints are usually stiff, and vibration can harden the wire and cause it to break. Solderless splices are designed to keep the joint flexible so vibration cannot cause the wire to break.

6. **What is the main disadvantage of aluminum wire over copper wire for use in an aircraft electrical system?**

   Aluminum wire is more brittle than copper. It is more subject to breakage when it is nicked or when it is subjected to vibration.

7. **What size aluminum wire would be proper to replace a piece of four-gage copper wire?**

   Two-gage. When you substitute aluminum wire for copper wire, use a wire that is two gage numbers larger.

8. **What is the smallest size aluminum wire that is approved for use in aircraft electrical systems?**

   Six-gage.

9. **What color insulator on a preinsulated solderless connector indicates that the connector is proper for a 10-gage wire?**

   Yellow.

Typical Practical Projects

1. Selecting the proper terminal and tools, install a solderless terminal on a piece of electrical wire furnished by the examiner.

2. Secure an electrical wire bundle to an aircraft structure using the proper clamps and grommets.

3. Demonstrate to the examiner the correct way to tie an electrical wire bundle with spot ties.

4. Splice an electrical wire, using the correct type of splice and the correct insulation.

5. Correctly attach wires to the terminals of a quick-disconnect connector.

6. Select and install the correct type of wiring in an electrical circuit.

7. Correctly install bonding jumpers.

D. Task: Adjust a Voltage Regulator

Reference: AMT-SYS, Chapter 7

Typical Oral Questions

1. **What size generator must be used in an aircraft electrical system if the connected electrical load is 30 amps, and there is no way of monitoring the generator output?**
   When monitoring is not practical, the total continuously connected electrical load must be no more than 80% of the rated generator output. This would require a generator with a rating of 37.5 amps. Practically, a 40-amp generator would be installed.

2. **What is meant by "flashing" the field of a generator?**
   Restoring the residual magnetism to the frame of the generator. This is done by passing battery current through the field coils in the direction it normally flows when the generator is operating.

3. **What is meant by paralleling the generators in a multi-engine aircraft?**
   Adjusting the voltage regulators so all the generators share the electrical load equally.

4. **What are three types of voltage regulators used with aircraft generators?**
   Vibrator-type, carbon-pile type, and solid state-type.

5. **How does a vibrator-type voltage regulator maintain a constant voltage?**

   When the voltage rises above the desired value, an electromagnetic relay opens and inserts a resistor in the generator field circuit, decreasing the field current and lowering the generator output voltage.

6. **What two components are normally housed with a vibrator voltage regulator in a single-unit generator control?**

   A current limiter and a reverse-current cutout relay.

Typical Practical Projects

1. Given the specifications of an aircraft generator, find its rated current output.

2. Explain to the examiner the correct way to flash the field of an aircraft generator.

3. Explain to the examiner the correct way to adjust the voltage controlled by a vibrator-type voltage regulator.

4. Explain to the examiner the way a carbon-pile voltage regulator operates and the way the paralleling circuit allows the generators to share the load equally.

E. Task: Inspect, Check, and Troubleshoot Aircraft Electrical Systems

Reference: AMT-SYS, Chapter 7

Typical Oral Questions

1. **Can you substitute aluminum wire for copper wire?**

   Yes. However you must use aluminum wire two wire gage sizes larger to carry the same current. Aluminum wire should never be used in runs of three feet or less, or in communication and navigation systems.

2. **Can wire in free air carry the same current as wire in a bundle?**

   Wire in free air may be used to a higher current level than the same size wire in a bundle. Always refer to an electrical wire size selection chart.

3. **What are common causes of wire failure in a crimped connector?**

   The wire was not inserted far enough into the connector and/or the connector was excessively crimped.

---

4. **What is one of the first things to check if an electrical component does not operate?**

   Always start with simple solutions and move to more complex. Is the component turned on? Is power available? For example, if a light doesn't function is the system turned on, is the aircraft electrical system energized, or is the bulb burnt out?

5. **What may be provided by the manufacturer to assist in troubleshooting?**

   Manufacturers often provide a troubleshooting logic chart.

6. **What are the four basic steps of troubleshooting?**

   Know how the system should operate. Observe the way the system is operating. Divide the system into smaller segments to isolate trouble. Look for the obvious problem first.

Typical Practical Projects

1. Determine an electrical load in a given aircraft system.

2. Check the resistance of an electrical system component.

3. Identify the components in an electrical system.

4. Identify the cockpit lighting circuits.

5. Identify the components in an electrical schematic where AC is rectified to a DC voltage.

6. Visually identify and describe operation of components in a constant speed drive (CSD) or integrated drive generator (IDG).

7. Check the generator brush spring tension and/or service ability.

8. Inspect and check anti-collision, position, and/or landing lights for proper operation.

9. Troubleshoot an electrical circuit with an open or short circuit.

10. Troubleshoot a DC electrical system supplied by an alternating current (AC) electrical system.

VIII. Area of Operation: Position and Warning System
A. Task: Adjust Landing Gear Position Switch

Reference: AMT-SYS, Chapter 10

Typical Oral Questions

1. What is a squat switch and where is it located?

A landing gear safety switch that energizes a circuit to prevent the landing gear retraction handle from being moved to the RETRACT position when weight is on the landing gear. It is located in the torsion links of one of the main landing gears.

2. What kind of device is normally used as a sensor to detect the condition of a retractable landing gear?

A precision Microswitch.

Typical Practical Projects

1. Demonstrate to the examiner the proper way to adjust landing gear position switches to the aircraft manufacturer's specifications.

2. Perform operational check of a retractable landing gear and explain to the examiner the interconnection between the landing gear position switches, the engine throttle(s) and the landing gear warning horn.

3. Make proper maintenance record entry for the completion of a landing gear retraction test.

4. Remove, install, and/or adjust a landing gear down-lock switch.

5. Check the rigging and adjustment of a landing gear up-lock.

B. Task: Adjust Flap Position Switch

Reference: AMT-SYS, Chapter 10

Typical Oral Questions

1. What type of system is used to indicate the position of the wing flaps?

Usually a resistance-type remote indicating system such as the DC Selsyn system.

2. What information is shown by the wing flap position indicator?

The number of degrees the flaps are lowered.

Typical Practical Projects

1. Demonstrate to the examiner the proper way to adjust the wing flap position sensors to the aircraft manufacturer's specifications.

2. Perform an operational check of the flaps and explain to the examiner the way to adjust the sensor to accurately indicate the position of the flaps.

3. Make proper maintenance record entry for the adjustment of the wing flap indicating system.

C. Task: Troubleshoot Landing Gear Warning System

Reference: AMT-SYS, Chapter 10

Typical Oral Questions

1. **What would cause the warning horn to sound when the throttles are pulled back, reducing the engine power for landing?**

   The warning horn will sound if any of the landing gears are not down and locked.

2. **What is indicated by a red light in the landing gear position-indication portion of the annunciator panel?**

   The red light indicates that the landing gear is not in a safe condition for landing.

3. **What information is given to a pilot to indicate that all of the landing gears are down and locked?**

   Three green lights are used on most aircraft to indicate that all three landing gears are down and locked.

Typical Practical Project

1. Using an electrical schematic diagram of a landing gear warning system, explain to the examiner what fault could prevent the system from warning of an unsafe landing gear condition.

D. Task: Repair Landing Gear Warning System

Reference: AMT-SYS, Chapter 10

Typical Oral Question

1. What is the most likely cause of a landing gear warning system failing to warn when the landing gear is not down and locked?
A faulty or misadjusted microswitch.

Typical Practical Projects

1. Perform operational check of a retractable landing gear and explain to the examiner the interconnection between the landing gear position switches, the engine throttle(s), and the landing gear warning horn.

2. Make proper maintenance record entry for the completion of a landing gear retraction test.

3. Identify the landing gear position system components.

4. Identify the landing gear warning system components.

5. Describe the sequence of operation for a landing gear warning system.

6. Locate the troubleshooting procedures for a takeoff warning system.

7 Troubleshoot the landing gear position and/or warning systems.

8. Inspect the landing gear position indicating system.

9. Repair the landing gear position indicating systems.

E. Task: Inspect, Check and Troubleshoot Brake Systems

Reference: AMT-STRUC, Chapter 6

Typical Oral Questions

1. What abnormal event warrants a special brake inspection?
If the aircraft experiences an aborted take-off or an emergency braking event occurs. These events cause excessive heating of brakes, wheels, and tires.

2. What is the likely cause of "spongy brakes"?
There are air bubbles in the brake lines.

---

3. **What are the two methods of bleeding brake systems?**
   Gravity and pressure bleeding.

4. **What condition exists when a brake locks on a water covered runway?**
   Hydroplaning.

5. **What is the likely cause of a dragging brake?**
   A warped disk.

6. **What is the function of a wheel speed sensor in a anti-skid brake system?**
   The wheel speed sensor is a DC generator that is used to produce a voltage proportional to wheel speed. Rotational speed change in excess of programmed parameters will engage the anti-skid data.

Typical Practical Projects

1. Locate procedures for checking operation of an anti-skid warning system.

2. Locate troubleshooting procedures for an anti-skid system.

3. Locate procedures for checking pneumatic/bleed air overheat warning systems.

4. Inspect an electrical brake control for proper operation.

IX. Area of Operation: Ice and Rain Control Systems

A. Task: Check and Troubleshoot an Electrically Heated Pitot System

Reference: AMT-SYS, Chapter 12

Typical Oral Questions

1. **How is ice kept from forming on the pitot tube of an airplane?**
   Pitot tubes are heated by electric current flowing through heater elements built into them.

2. **How can you tell, on a preflight inspection, that the pitot heater is operating?**
   Turn it on for about a minute and then on the walk-around inspection, feel it to see that it is warm.

Typical Practical Project

1. Actuate a pitot heater and check it for proper operation.

2. Locate the procedures for troubleshooting an electrically heated pitot system.

B. Task: Replace Electrically Heated Pitot Tube

Reference: AMT-SYS, Chapter 12

Typical Oral Questions

1. **Where can you find the correct part number for the electrically heated pitot head used on an aircraft?**
   In the illustrated parts manual for the aircraft.

2. **If the pitot head includes ports for the static air system, what must be done after the head is replaced?**
   A static system leak test must be performed and the results recorded in the aircraft maintenance records.

Typical Practical Projects

1. Locate the part number for a pitot head and explain to the examiner the way the head would be replaced.

2. Perform an operational check of the replaced pitot head.

3. Make an entry of the replaced pitot head in the aircraft maintenance records.

C. Task: Repair a Pneumatic Deicer Boot

Reference: AMT-SYS, Chapter 12

Typical Oral Questions

1. **Why is it important that ice not be allowed to build up on airplane wings in flight?**
   Ice distorts the shape of the airfoil and destroys the aerodynamic lift. The weight of the ice loads the aircraft down.

2. Are pneumatic deicer boots operated before ice forms, or after it has formed?

Pneumatic deicer boots are not operated until ice has formed over them. When the boot inflates, it breaks the ice, and the air flowing over the airfoil blows it away.

3. Where does the air come from to operate the pneumatic deicer boots on a reciprocating-engine powered airplane?

From the discharge side of the air pump used to operate the gyro instruments.

4. What is meant by a wet vacuum pump?

It is a vacuum pump that uses engine oil to lubricate its steel vanes. A dry vacuum pump uses carbon vanes, and it does not require any oil for lubrication.

5. What is the purpose of the oil separator in a deicer system?

Oil separators are used with wet vacuum pumps to remove the lubricating oil from the discharge air before this air is used in the deicer boots.

6. How are rubber deicer boots cleaned?

By washing them with mild soap and water.

7. How are rubber deicer boots attached to the leading edges of aircraft wings and tail surfaces?

They are bonded to the surface with an adhesive. Boots on the older aircraft were attached with machine screws and Rivnuts.

Typical Practical Projects

1. Demonstrate to the examiner the correct way to patch a pneumatic deicer boot following the instructions of the boot manufacturer.

2. Perform an operational check of the deicer system, explaining to the examiner the purpose of the sequencing of the inflation of the boots.

3. Inspect a pneumatic deicer boot.

4. Clean a pneumatic deicer boot.

D. Task: Rain Control

Reference: AMT-SYS, Chapter 12

Typical Oral Questions

1. **How is ice prevented from forming on the windshield of modern jet transport airplanes?**

   The windshield has a heater element embedded in it. Electric current heats the windshield and keeps ice from forming on it.

2. **What are two ways rain can be kept from obstructing the pilot's vision through the windshield of an airplane?**

   The rain can be blown away by a high velocity blast of compressor bleed air, or it can be wiped away with electrically or hydraulically operated windshield wipers.

3. **When should rain repellent be used on an airplane windshield?**

   Only when the windshield is wet with rain.

4. **Where can you find the instructions for adjusting the tension for the windshield wiper blades?**

   In the aircraft maintenance manual.

Typical Practical Projects

1. Examine the blades of a windshield wiper system, and check them for the correct tension and for the correct parking position.

2. Locate and identify the containers of chemical rain repellent.

3. Replace blades on a windshield wiper system.

4. Check pneumatic rain removal system.

5. Locate inspection procedures for chemical rain protection of a windscreen.

6. Check an electrically or hydraulically operated windshield wiper system.

E. Task: Inspect and Check Anti-Ice Systems

Reference: AMT-SYS, Chapter 12

Typical Oral Questions

1. **How can you test if the pitot heat is working?**
   Briefly turn the pitot heat system on and observe an increased current indication on the ammeter.

2. **What is the sequence of inflation of a deicing boot system?**
   There are three tubes in a deicer boot, upper, center, and lower. The center tube inflates first with the upper and lower tubes a specified number of seconds later.

3. **What might be likely causes for a propeller electrothermal deicer system failure?**
   A tripped circuit breaker or broken wire to the electrical heating elements.

4. **How can a pilot determine if an electrothermal propeller deicer is working?**
   The pilot should observe an increased ammeter reading when the system is energized.

Typical Practical Projects

1. Check an electrically heated water drain system.

2. Inspect the thermal anti-ice systems.

3. Check an electrically heated windshield.

4. Inspect an electrically operated windshield wiper system.

X. Area of Operation: Fire Protection Systems
A. Task: Fire Detection and Indication Systems

Reference: AMT-SYS, Chapter 13

Typical Oral Questions

1. **What is a Class B fire?**
   Class B fires are those caused by combustable fluids.

2. **What type of fire detection system is usually used in engine compartments, APU installations, and wheel wells?**
   A continuous-loop fire detection system.

---

3. What type of detector is commonly used in baggage compartments and holds?

Smoke detectors.

4. What type of detector is usually used in the cockpit and cabin areas?

CO detectors.

5. What are the three elements required for a fire?

Fuel, oxygen, and high enough temperature.

Typical Practical Projects

1. Locate the inspection procedures for carbon monoxide detectors.

2. Locate the procedures for checking a smoke detection system.

3. Locate the procedures for inspecting a thermal switch fire detection system.

4. Inspect, check, troubleshoot, and/or repair a fire detection system.

5. Inspect a thermocouple fire warning system.

6. Check a continuous loop fire detection system.

7. Inspect a continuous loop fire detection system.

8. Check a Freon bottle discharge circuit.

B. Task: Fire Extinguisher Container Pressure Check

Reference: AMT-SYS, Chapter 13

Typical Oral Questions

1. What type of fire extinguishing agent is best for both cabin fires and engine fires?

Halon 1301.

2. What is a major disadvantage of "CB" fire extinguishing agent for extinguishing aircraft fires?

It is corrosive to aluminum and magnesium.

3. Why is carbon tetrachloride not recommended as a fire extinguishing agent?

Carbon tetrachloride produces phosgene, a deadly gas, when it is exposed to flames.

---

4. **What is used as a fire extinguishing agent in most of the high-rate discharge systems installed in aircraft?**

   One of the halogenated hydrocarbons, such as Halon 1301, pressurized with nitrogen.

5. **How can you determine the state of charge of a CO_2 fire extinguisher?**

   By its weight.

6. **How can you determine the state of charge of a freon fire extinguisher container?**

   By the pressure shown on the built-in gage.

7. **How does the ambient temperature effect the pressure shown on the pressure gage on a freon fire extinguisher?**

   The higher the temperature, the higher the pressure.

Typical Practical Project

1. Demonstrate to the examiner the correct way to check the pressure on a high-rate discharge fire extinguisher container. Explain the reason for the allowable pressure range.

C. Task: Inspect Fire Extinguisher Bottle or Cylinder

Reference: AMT-SYS, Chapter 13

Typical Oral Questions

1. **What releases the fire extinguishing agent in a high-rate discharge bottle?**

   An electrically ignited powder charge blows a knife through a seal in the HRD bottle.

2. **What precaution must you observe when checking the electrical squib of an HRD fire extinguisher bottle for electrical continuity?**

   It takes only a small amount of current to ignite the powder charge, and the method of testing must not send this amount of current through it.

Typical Practical Projects

1. Demonstrate to the examiner the correct way to determine the state of charge of a CO_2 fire extinguisher bottle.

2. Inspect the fire protection system CO_2 cylinders.

3. Inspect a conventional CO_2 fire protection system.

4. Check a conventional CO_2 fire protection system.

5. Check a fire protection system Freon bottle charge pressure.

6. Inspect a Freon bottle discharge cartridge.

7. Inspect a fire-extinguisher bottle or cylinder for hydrostatic test date.

D. Task: Troubleshoot Fire Detection System

Reference: AMT-SYS, Chapter 13

Typical Oral Questions

1. Does a thermocouple fire detection system warn the pilot of a general overheat condition?

No, it operates on the rate of temperature rise, and it detects only a fire.

2. Does a thermal switch fire detection warn the pilot of a general overheat condition?

No, it actuates only when there is a fire.

3. How is a thermoswitch fire detector circuit checked?

Close the test switch. If the system is continuous and not shorted, the fire-warning light and bell will actuate. Failure of the warning light to illuminate shows the system is faulty.

4. How is a continuous-loop fire detector circuit checked?

Close the test switch. If the system is continuous and not shorted, the fire-warning light and bell will actuate. Failure of the warning light to illuminate shows the system is faulty.

5. Does a pneumatic fire detection system warn the pilot of a general overheat condition?

Yes, it actuates when there is a fire or a general overheat condition.

6. How is the pneumatic fire detection system tested?

When the test switch is closed, low-voltage AC flows through the stainless steel tube in which the gas absorbing element is housed. This current heats the element which releases gas and actuates the fire warning light and bell.

Typical Practical Project

1. Given a schematic diagram of a fire detection system, describe to the examiner faults that could cause a false alarm, and faults that could prevent the system indicating the presence of a fire.

2. Locate the troubleshooting procedures for a high rate of discharge fire extinguisher system.

E. Task: Service Fire Extinguisher System

Reference: AMT-SYS, Chapter 13

Typical Oral Questions

1. **What happens when the Fire-Pull T-handle is pulled in a jet transport aircraft?**

   The bottle discharge switch is uncovered and armed, the generator field relay is tripped, fuel is shut off to the engine, and hydraulic fluid is shut off to the pump. The engine bleed air is shut off and the hydraulic pump low-pressure lights are deactivated.

2. **What must be done to release the fire extinguishing agent after the Fire-Pull T-handle has been pulled?**

   The Bottle Discharge switch must be closed.

3. **What type of fire extinguisher is recommended for extinguishing a brake fire?**

   A dry-powder type extinguisher.

4. **How can you determine whether or not a built-in fire extinguishing system has been discharged?**

   By checking the blowout plugs on the outside of the aircraft near the extinguisher agent bottles.

5. **What is indicated if the red disk in a built-in fire extinguishing system is blown out?**

   The agent bottle has been discharged because of an overheat condition.

6. **What is indicated if the yellow disk in a built-in fire extinguishing system is blown out?**

   The agent bottle has been discharged by the flight crew actuating the Bottle Discharge switch.

Typical Practical Projects

1. Inspect an HRD fire extinguishing system for security of its components and for the state of charge of its bottles.

2. Explain to the examiner the way the electrical circuit for an HRD fire extinguishing system should be checked.

3. Locate and identify the blow-out plugs that indicate the status of the fire extinguisher system in an aircraft.

4. Demonstrate to the examiner the correct way to remove and replace an HRD fire extinguishing agent container.

The Powerplant Oral and Practical Tests

There are 15 Areas of Operation that are tested on the Powerplant Oral and Practical tests.

Following this list are the suggested study areas, typical oral questions with succinct answers and typical practical projects for each area of operation.

A. Reciprocating Engines
   1. Inspect and repair radial engines
   2. Inspect, check, service, troubleshoot and repair reciprocating engines and engine installations
   3. Install and remove reciprocating engines

B. Turbine Engines
   1. Inspect, check, service, troubleshoot and repair turbine engines and engine installations

C. Engine Inspection
   1. Perform powerplant airworthiness inspection

D. Engine Instrument Systems
   1. Troubleshoot and repair electrical rate-of-fluid-flow indicating systems for turbine engines
   2. Inspect, check, troubleshoot, and repair electrical and mechanical engine temperature, pressure and RPM indicating systems

E. Engine Fire Protection Systems
   1. Inspect, check, troubleshoot, and repair engine fire detection and extinguishing systems

F. Engine Electrical Systems
   1. Repair engine electrical system components
   2. Install, check, and repair engine electrical wiring, controls, switches, indicators, and protective devices

G. Lubrication Systems
   1. Identify and select lubricants
   2. Inspect, check, service, troubleshoot, and repair engine lubrication systems

H. Ignition and Starting Systems
   1. Inspect, troubleshoot, and repair reciprocating and turbine engine ignition systems
   2. Inspect, troubleshoot, and repair turbine engine electrical starting systems
   3. Inspect, troubleshoot, and repair turbine engine pneumatic starting systems

I. Fuel Metering Systems
   1. Troubleshoot and adjust turbine engine fuel metering systems and electronic engine fuel controls

J. Engine Fuel Systems
   1. Inspect, check, troubleshoot, and repair reciprocating and turbine engine fuel systems

K. Induction and Engine Airflow Systems
   1. Inspect, check, troubleshoot, and repair engine ice control systems
   2. Inspect, check, and repair carburetor air intake systems and induction manifolds

L. Engine Cooling Systems
   1. Inspect, check, troubleshoot, and repair engine cooling systems

M. Engine Exhaust and Thrust Reverser Systems
   1. Inspect, check, troubleshoot, and repair engine exhaust, heat exchangers, and turbocharger systems
   2. Troubleshoot and repair engine thrust reverser systems and related components

N. Propellers
   1. Inspect, check, and repair propeller synchronizing and ice control systems
   2. Identify and select propeller lubricants
   3. Inspect, check, service, and repair fixed pitch, constant speed and feathering propellers and propeller governing systems
   4. Install, troubleshoot, and remove propellers
   5. Inspect and repair aluminum alloy propeller blades

O. Turbine-Powered Auxiliary Power Units
   1. Inspect, check, service, and troubleshoot turbine-driven auxiliary power units

Area of Operation: A. Reciprocating Engines

A01. Task: Inspection and Repair of Radial Engine

Reference: AMT-P, Chapters 2 and 9

Typical Oral Questions

1. **In what position should the crankshaft be when a magneto is being timed to the engine?**

   The piston in cylinder no. 1 should be in the correct position for ignition to occur. This is normally about 30° before top center on the compression stroke.

2. **What is the purpose of a cold cylinder check?**

   A cold cylinder check determines which cylinder is not firing. Run the engine for a few minutes at the speed, and on the magneto, at which it runs roughest. Shut it down and feel the exhaust stack near the cylinder head. The cylinder with the stack that is not as hot as the others is the cylinder that has not been firing.

3. **What is checked on engine runup to determine the operational condition of the engine?**

   Idling RPM and manifold pressure, engine acceleration, maximum static RPM and manifold pressure, magneto drop, ignition switch safety check, propeller pitch change, propeller feathering, oil pressure, fuel pressure, and fuel flow.

4. **How can you determine the firing order of an 18-cylinder radial engine?**

   Begin with cylinder 1, add 11 and subtract 7, whichever will keep the numbers between 1 and 18. 1-12-5-16-9-2-13-6-17-10-3-14-7-18-11-4-15-8.

5. **What are two main causes of a cylinder having low compression?**

   Piston rings not seating or broken, and valves not seating or burned.

6. **What is a hydraulic lock in an aircraft engine?**

   Oil has drained past the piston rings and filled the combustion chamber of cylinders that are below the center line of the engine. If the crankshaft is turned over with this oil in the cylinder it will lock, and there is a probability that the piston, cylinder, or connecting rod will be damaged.

7. **How is a hydraulic lock removed from an aircraft engine?**

   Remove a spark plug from the locked cylinder and drain all of the oil out. Clean the spark plug and replace it.

8. What is a low-tension ignition system?

It is an ignition system using a magneto with a brush-type distributor and a coil that has no secondary wiring. Low voltage is directed from the magneto to a transformer mounted on the cylinder head. Here the low voltage is boosted to a high voltage and is directed through a very short high-tension lead to the spark plug. There is one transformer for each spark plug.

9. What is a floating cam ring on a large radial engine?

It is a cam ring that rides on a shelf-type bearing with a large amount of clearance between the bearing and the ring. When adjusting the valves on an engine with a floating cam ring, the pressure of the valve springs on the opposite side of the engine must be removed so the cam ring will be tight against the bearing for the valves being adjusted.

10. Why is valve clearance adjusted on radial engines, but not on most horizontally opposed engines?

Most horizontally opposed engines have hydraulic valve lifters that keep all of the clearance out of the valve train. Radial engines have solid lifters.

11. Why are both the hot and cold valve clearances given for most radial engines?

The hot clearance is given for valve timing purposes. The timing is adjusted with the valves in cylinder number one, set with the hot clearance. When the timing is set, all of the valves are adjusted to their cold clearance.

A02. Task: Inspect, Check, Service, Troubleshoot and Repair Reciprocating Engines and Engine Installations

Reference: AMT-P, Chapters 2 and 9

Typical Oral Questions

1. What must be inspected to determine the airworthiness of an engine installation?

The propeller, lubrication system, ignition system, fuel metering system, cooling system, and the exhaust system.

2. What checks should be made to determine the proper operation of a reciprocating engine installation?

Idle RPM and mixture, static RPM, propeller pitch change operation, magneto check, ignition switch safety check, and carburetor heat check.

3. Where can you find the correct grade of fuel and amount of engine lubricating oil for an aircraft engine?

In the Type Certificate Data Sheets for the aircraft.

4. What are the basic steps in troubleshooting an engine installation?

a. *Know how the system should operate.*

b. *Observe how the system is operating.*

c. *Divide the system to find the trouble.*

d. *Look for the obvious problems first.*

5. Where do you find the procedures to follow when correcting a defective condition in an aircraft engine?

In the engine maintenance manual.

Typical Practical Projects

1. Demonstrate the correct way to replace the packing seals around a push rod housing.

2. Demonstrate to the examiner the way to check an engine fuel system for leaks using pressure from the auxiliary fuel pump.

3. Perform an engine runup to determine that the engine is operating according to the engine manufacturer's specifications. Explain to the examiner what should be checked on this runup.

4. Perform a 100-hour inspection of an aircraft engine. Explain to the examiner the way you determined that this installation meets the specifications of the aircraft manufacturer. Make an entry in the aircraft records of the inspection.

5. Check the timing of the magnetos to the engine and determine whether or not this timing is within the limits allowed by the engine manufacturer.

6. Perform a differential compression test on an engine specified by the examiner. Explain to the examiner what could cause low compression on one or more cylinders, and what action could be taken to correct the situation.

7. Check all of the engine controls for proper travel and free motion. Explain to the examiner the reason for rigging the controls so they have some cushion.

8. Demonstrate the correct way to adjust the oil pressure on an engine specified by the examiner.

9. Demonstrate the correct way to adjust the idle speed and mixture on an engine specified by the examiner.

Continued

---

10. Service the lubrication system of an engine specified by the examiner. Inspect the filter and identify the source of the various types of contaminants. Install a new filter, fill the oil reservoir with the correct type and amount of oil and perform a check for oil leaks.

11. Explain to the examiner the way a cylinder should be inspected and repaired if the differential compression check identifies a leak past the valves.

12. Remove a cylinder. Inspect the cylinder and identify the parts and describe your findings to the examiner. Properly reinstall the cylinder.

13. Remove and replace a stud.

14. Install the piston and/or knuckle pin(s).

15. Identify the parts of a crankshaft and perform a dimensional inspection.

16. Identify and inspect various types of bearings.

17. Adjust the valve clearances.

18. Inspect the engine mounts.

19. Perform a cold cylinder check.

A03. Task: Install and Remove Reciprocating Engines

Reference: AMT-P, Chapters 2 and 9

Typical Oral Questions

1. **Where do you find instructions for removing an engine from an aircraft?**
   In the aircraft maintenance manual.

2. **What must normally be done to a nose-wheel airplane before removing an engine?**
   The tail of the airplane must be supported.

3. **What should be done to the cylinders to protect them from rust and corrosion when preparing the engine for long-time storage?**
   Spray a preservative oil inside the cylinders and replace the spark plugs with desiccant plugs.

4. **What should be used to cover the ends of fuel and oil lines that have been disconnected from the engine?**

   The correct plugs or caps. Never cover the end of a line with tape.

5. **What is meant by a QEC engine assembly?**

   An engine that has been prepared for a quick engine change. The engine is on its mount and all of the accessories are installed. A minimum of time is required to change engines. All that is needed is for the controls, wiring, and fluid lines to be connected to the firewall.

6. **What is meant by rigging the engine controls so they have some "cushion"?**

   The control on the engine component must contact its stop before the control handle in the cockpit reaches its stop. This causes the control handle to spring back a slight amount when it is moved to the extent of its travel.

7. **What are two ways of pre-oiling an engine?**

   a. *Before the spark plugs are installed and after the oil tank or sump is filled, turn the engine over with the starter until oil runs out of the fitting to which the oil pressure gage connects.*

   b. *Use a pre-oiler tank. Air pressure forces oil through all of the passages until some of it flows from the oil pressure gage fitting.*

Area of Operation: B. Turbine Engines

B01. Task: Inspect, Check, Troubleshoot and Repair Turbine Engines and Turbine Engine Installations

Reference: AMT-P, Chapters 10 and 15

Typical Oral Questions

1. **What is meant by a hot-section inspection?**

   An inspection of the hot section of a turbine engine. The hot section includes the combustors, the turbine, and the exhaust system.

2. **What is meant by on-condition maintenance of a turbine engine?**

   The monitoring of the engine performance at regular intervals and determining when maintenance is required based on certain operating parameters specified by the engine manufacturer.

3. **What checks of a turbine engine are necessary to verify preflight condition?**

   * *Inspection of the cowling and all air inlet areas and attachment of the engine to the airframe.*
   * *Inspection of the inlet guide vanes and the first stage of the compressor or fan blades.*

Continued

- *Check for unusual noise when the compressor is rotated.*
- *Inspection of the rear turbine, and exhaust system.*
- *Check the quantity of the lubricating oil for the engine and the constant-speed drive unit.*
- *Check the ignition system for operation by listening for the sparks.*

4. What is meant by trimming a turbine engine?

Adjusting the fuel control so the engine develops the correct idle and trim speed RPM.

5. What type of equipment should be used to determine that a turbine engine is performing up to the standards specified by the engine manufacturer?

A JetCal Analyzer/Trimmer has all of the instrumentation and cables to determine the EGT, EPR, and the other parameters specified by the engine manufacturer.

Typical Practical Projects

1. Demonstrate to the examiner the correct way to examine the compressor section of a turbine engine for evidence of FOD.

2. Demonstrate the correct way to install and connect a fuel nozzle in a turbine engine specified by the examiner.

3. Demonstrate the correct way to use a borescope to examine the condition of a turbine blade in an engine specified by the examiner.

4. Repair a turbine blade by blending out the damaged area. Check with the appropriate documentation to determine the maximum amount of the blade material that may be removed.

5. Demonstrate the correct way to perform a prestart inspection on a turbine engine designated by the examiner.

6. Demonstrate to the examiner the proper way to inspect a turbine engine installation to ensure that the engine and its accessories are installed in accordance with the manufacturer's specifications.

7. Demonstrate the correct way to determine the allowable cycle life of a turbine engine component specified by the examiner.

8. Demonstrate the correct way to remove, check, and replace an engine bleed air valve on the engine specified by the examiner.

9. Given the operating records of a turbine engine, demonstrate the way to calculate the cycle life between overhauls of a component specified by the examiner.

Continued

Aviation Maintenance Technician

10. Given one or more turbine blades and the appropriate maintenance manual, demonstrate the correct way to measure the blades.

11. Demonstrate to the examiner the correct way to start a turbine engine. Explain the way to detect a hot start and a hung start, and the correct procedure to follow if either occurs.

12. Identify the characteristics of different turbine compressors.

13. Identify the types of turbine blades.

14. Identify the major components of turbine engines.

15. Identify the airflow direction and pressure changes in turbojet engines.

16. Remove and install a combustion case and liner.

17. Inspect the combustion liners.

18. Locate the procedures for the adjustment of a fuel control unit.

19. Perform a turbine engine inlet guide vane and compressor blade inspection.

20. Locate the procedures for trimming a turbine engine.

21. Identify the causes for engine performance loss.

22. Remove and/or install a turbine rotor disk.

23. Identify damaged inlet nozzle guide vanes.

Area of Operation: C. Engine Inspection

C01. Task: Perform Powerplant Airworthiness Inspection

References: AC 43.13-1B; 14 CFR Part 43, Appendix D

Typical Oral Questions

1. **Where can you find the model of magneto that is approved for an engine specified by the examiner?**
   In the Type Certificate Data Sheet for the engine.

2. **What is a Supplemental Type Certificate?**
   An approval issued by the FAA for a modification to a type-certificated airframe, engine or component.

3. **What paperwork is necessary for the installation of a magneto that was not approved for an engine when it was certificated, but is approved for the engine when installed according to an STC?**

A form FAA 337 must be completed stating that the installation was done in accordance with the specific STC.

Typical Practical Projects

1. Conduct a 100-hour inspection on an aircraft engine specified by the examiner using the checklist prepared by the aircraft manufacturer.

2. Check the records of an engine specified by the examiner for a list of all of the applicable airworthiness directives. Explain to the examiner the way a specific AD should be complied with, and write up a maintenance record entry for the compliance.

3. Explain to the examiner the changes in an inspection program caused by a modification that was done according to an airworthiness directive.

4. Identify an engine type without reference material other than the data plate.

5. Determine engine conformity with engine specifications or type certificate data sheet.

6. Check the engine controls for freedom of operation.

7. Inspect an engine for fluid leaks after performing maintenance.

8. Inspect an aircraft engine's accessories for conformity.

9. Inspect an aircraft engine for service bulletin compliance.

10. Inspect an aircraft turbine engine for records time left on any life limited parts.

11. Perform an over temperature inspection.

12. Perform an engine over torque inspection.

13. Perform an aircraft engine over speed inspection.

14. Determine the conformity of installed spark plugs or igniters.

15. Determine if an aircraft engine's maintenance manual is current.

Area of Operation: D. Engine Instrument Systems

D01. Task: Troubleshoot and Repair Turbine Engine Electrical Rate-of-Fluid-Flow Indicating Systems

Reference: AMT-P, Chapter 16

Typical Oral Questions

1. **What are three types of flow-indicating systems used for turbine engines?**
   Vane-type flow meters, synchronous mass-type flow meters, and electronic motorless mass flow meters.

2. **What do mass flow systems measure?**
   The mass of the flow. This is affected by the density of the fuel which is in turn affected by the fuel temperature.

3. **In what units is an electronic motorless mass flow meter system calibrated?**
   Pounds per hour of fuel flow.

4. **What is indicated in a turbine engine if the fuel flow for all conditions is high?**
   If there are other instrument abnormalities, there are possibly damaged turbine components.

5. **Who is authorized to repair a fuel flow indicating system?**
   The components can be repaired only by an FAA approved repair station certificated for the particular instruments.

6. **Where can you find the electrical power requirements for a fuel flow indicating system?**
   In the aircraft maintenance manual.

7. **Where in the fuel system is the fuel flow transmitter located?**
   Between the fuel control and the fuel nozzles.

D02. Task: Inspect, Check, Troubleshoot, and Repair Electrical and Mechanical Engine Temperature, Pressure, and RPM Indicating Systems

Reference: AMT-P, Chapter 16

Typical Oral Questions

1. **What kind of indicating system is used to measure oil temperature in a small, single-engine, general aviation airplane?**

   A sealed system in which a bulb, partially filled with a highly volatile liquid, is installed inside the oil strainer. The bulb is connected to a pressure gage by a copper tube. The pressure of the gas above the liquid is proportional to the temperature of the oil that surrounds the bulb, and the pressure gage is calibrated in terms of temperature.

2. **What type of instrument system is used for measuring cylinder-head temperature and exhaust gas temperature?**

   A thermocouple system.

3. **What kind of electrical instrument system is used for measuring oil temperature?**

   A ratiometer-type system.

4. **What should a thermocouple cylinder-head temperature indicator read when the engine is cold?**

   The same as the outside air temperature gage.

5. **What is critical in the installation of the thermocouple leads for a cylinder-head temperature indicator, the length of the leads or their resistance?**

   The resistance is critical, it must have the resistance specified on the indicator. This is usually 2 or 8 ohms.

6. **What should a ratiometer temperature indicator read when the electrical power is off?**

   The pointer should be off scale on the low side.

7. **What kind of tachometer is used on most small single-engine airplanes?**

   A magnetic drag tachometer that is similar to an automobile speedometer.

8. **What would likely cause the pointer of a magnetic drag tachometer to oscillate?**

   Either a dry cable connecting the indicator to the engine, or a kink in the cable housing.

9. **Is it permissible for a mechanic with an airframe and powerplant rating to replace the tachometer cable for a magnetic drag tachometer?**

   Yes, this does not constitute a repair to an instrument.

10. **What kind of tachometer is used on most large multi-engine airplanes?**
    A three-phase AC electric tachometer.

11. **What is measured to indicate the engine RPM with a three-phase AC electric tachometer?**
    The frequency of the AC the tachometer generator produces.

12. **What kind of indicator mechanism is used to measure oil pressure?**
    A Bourdon tube.

13 **What kind of indicator mechanism is used to measure manifold pressure?**
    A differential bellows.

14. **What should a manifold pressure gage read when the engine is not operating?**
    The existing barometric pressure as indicated on the altimeter barometric scale when the altimeter pointers are set to the surveyed field elevation.

15. **What type of fitting is used to connect an oil pressure gage to the engine?**
    A fitting with a restrictor that smoothes out the pulsations and prevents a break in the indicator line, causing a serious loss of engine oil.

16. **What is used to fill the line between a fuel pressure gage and the fuel metering system?**
    A light oil such as kerosine.

17. **What could cause a fuel pressure gage to fluctuate?**
    The loss of the light oil in the line between the gage and the engine.

18. **Is a certificated mechanic with an airframe and powerplant rating allowed to zero the pointers on a fuel pressure gage?**
    No, a mechanic is not allowed to make any repairs or alterations to an aircraft instrument.

19. **How does a ratiometer-type oil temperature gage measure the temperature of the oil?**
    A ratiometer measures the resistance of the temperature bulb. The indicator is calibrated in degrees Fahrenheit or Celsius rather than in ohms.

20. **What is the range of pressure needed for a fuel pressure gage used with a float carburetor?**
    Normally from 1 to 25 psi.

Typical Practical Projects

1. Demonstrate to the examiner the way to check all the components in a cylinder-head temperature indicating system.

2. Demonstrate to the examiner the way to check the capillary tube that connects a mechanical oil temperature gage to the engine.

3. Demonstrate the way to check or replace the tachometer cable for a magnetic drag tachometer.

4. Locate and identify the tachometer generator on an engine specified by the examiner.

5. Locate and identify the oil temperature bulb on an engine specified by the examiner. Explain the precautions to be taken when replacing the bulb.

6. Explain to the examiner the troubleshooting procedure for an oscillating cylinder-head temperature indicator.

7. Demonstrate to the examiner the way to replace a thermocouple probe for a cylinder-head temperature indicating system.

8. Demonstrate to the examiner the way to check an electric tachometer system for a failure of the system to indicate.

9. Remove, inspect, and/or install a fuel-flow transmitter.

10. Remove, inspect, and/or install a fuel flow gage.

11. Identify the various components installed on an engine.

12. Check the fuel flow transmitter power supply.

13. Troubleshoot a fuel-flow system.

14. Inspect a tachometer's markings for accuracy.

15. Remove, inspect, and/or install a turbine engine exhaust gas temperature (EGT) harness.

16. Troubleshoot a turbine engine pressure ratio (EPR) system.

17. Replace a cylinder head temperature thermocouple.

18. Locate and inspect an engine's low fuel pressure warning system components.

Continued

19. Check an aircraft engine manifold pressure gage for proper operation.

20. Inspect a leaking manifold pressure system.

21. Repair a low oil pressure warning system.

22. Troubleshoot an EGT indicating system.

Area of Operation: F. Engine Fire Protection Systems
E01. Task: Inspect, Check, Troubleshoot, and Repair Engine Fire Detection and Extinguishing Systems

Reference: AMT-P, Chapter 18

Typical Oral Questions

1. **What are four types of engine fire detection systems?**
   Thermoswitch system, thermocouple system, thermistor-type continuous-loop system, pneumatic-type continuous-loop system.

2. **Which type of fire detection system operates on the principle of the rate of temperature rise?**
   The thermocouple system.

3. **Why must the reference junction in a thermocouple fire detection system be thermally insulated?**
   This is a rate-of-temperature-rise system. The reference junction must be insulated so its temperature will not rise as quickly as that of the measuring junctions if a fire should occur.

4. **How do you check a thermocouple fire detection system for operation?**
   Press the test switch. This heats the test thermocouple enough for it to close the sensitive relay, which in turn closes the slave relay and activates the fire warning light and bell.

5. **What would likely cause a false fire alarm in a thermistor-type continuous-loop system?**
   A kinked or pinched continuous-loop element.

6. **If there is a break in a single-wire continuous-loop fire detector element, and the system tests bad, will it indicate the presence of a fire?**
   Yes, even though it tests bad, it will still indicate the presence of a fire.

7. **How is a pneumatic-type continuous-loop fire detection system checked for operation?**

   When the test switch is closed, low-voltage AC flows through the tube that encloses the sensitive element. This current heats the element enough for it to release sufficient gas to activate the alarm switch.

8. **What maintenance is allowed on a continuous-loop fire detection system?**

   Inspect and replace as needed the continuous-loop element, the controller, and the fire warning bell and/or light.

9. **What happens in a jet transport airplane when the fire-pull T-handle for an engine is pulled?**

   The engine fuel shutoff valve is closed.
   The generator field relay is tripped.
   The compressor bleed air valve is closed.
   The anti-ice valve is closed.
   The hydraulic supply shutoff valve is closed.
   The hydraulic pump low-pressure warning lights are turned off.

10. **What is used as a fire extinguishing agent in some older aircraft?**

    Carbon dioxide (CO_2).

11. **What fire extinguishing agent is used in the high-rate discharge bottles installed in a jet transport aircraft?**

    Halon 1211 or 1301.

12. **How is a high-rate discharge bottle of fire extinguishing agent discharged?**

    A powder charge is ignited and it blows a cutter through a frangible disk that seals the bottle.

13. **What precaution must be taken when checking the electrical circuit for igniting the powder charge in the valve of a high-rate discharge bottle?**

    The current used to check the integrity of the electric circuit must not be high enough to ignite the powder charge.

14. **What is indicated if the red discharge indicator for a fire extinguishing system is blown out?**

    The system has been discharged by an overheat condition.

15. **What is indicated if the yellow discharge indicator for a fire extinguishing system is blown out?**

    The system has been discharged by actuating the bottle discharge switch.

16. What color and marking is used to identify the fluid lines that carry the fire extinguishing agent in an aircraft?

Brown tape with a series of diamonds on it.

Typical Practical Projects

1. Demonstrate to the examiner the correct way to determine the state of charge of a CO_2 fire extinguisher bottle.

2. Demonstrate to the examiner the correct way to determine the state of charge of an HRD fire extinguisher bottle.

3. Demonstrate to the examiner the correct way to check a continuous-loop fire detection system for integrity.

4. Demonstrate the correct way to attach a section of continuous-loop fire detection element to the aircraft structure.

5. Identify to the examiner the valves that are shut off when the fire-pull T-handle is pulled.

6. Demonstrate to the examiner the way to check the squib in a high-rate-discharge bottle of fire extinguishing agent for the shelf-life date.

7. Identify the fire detection sensing units.

8. Inspect the fire detection continuous loop system.

9. Inspect a fire detection thermal switch or thermocouple system.

10. Check and/or inspect a fire detection warning system.

11. Locate the troubleshooting information for a fire detection system.

12. Inspect a turbine engine fire detection system.

13. Inspect an engine's fire extinguisher system blowout plugs.

14. Check the fire extinguisher discharge circuit.

15. Troubleshoot a fire protection system.

16. Inspect a fire extinguisher system for hydrostatic test requirements.

17. Check the flame detectors for operation.

Continued

Area of Operation: F. Engine Electrical Systems

F01. Task: Repair Engine Electrical System Components

Reference: AMT-P, Chapter 17

Typical Oral Questions

1. **When should the brushes in a starter motor be replaced?**
   When they have worn to one half of their original length.

2. **How is the direction of rotation of a DC electric motor reversed?**
   Reverse the polarity of the armature or the field, but not both.

3. **What is used as the rectifier to produce direct current in a DC generator?**
   Brushes and a commutator.

4. **What is used as the rectifier to produce direct current in a DC alternator?**
   Six solid-state diodes.

5. **Is a starter motor series-wound or shunt-wound?**
   Series wound for maximum stalled-rotor torque.

6. **What are two ways wires can be attached to the pins in a cannon plug?**
   a. *By soldering the wires into pots on the pins and sockets.*
   b. *By crimping tapered pins onto the wires and inserting the pins into tapered holes in the pins and sockets.*

7. **Why is stranded wire used rather than solid wire, in most powerplant electrical systems?**
   Solid wire is likely to break when it is subjected to vibration.

8. **What two things must be considered in selection of wire size when making an electrical installation in an aircraft?**
   The current-carrying capability of the wire, and the voltage drop caused by current flowing through the wire.

9. **What must be done to a DC generator, after it has been overhauled, before it can produce electricity?**

The field must be flashed to restore residual magnetism to the field frame so it can begin to produce current.

10. **Why is it not necessary to flash the field of a DC alternator after it has been overhauled?**

An alternator field is excited by battery current and residual voltage is not used to start the alternator producing current.

Typical Practical Projects

1. Use publications to determine replacement part numbers.

2. Replace an engine-driven generator or alternator.

3. Parallel a dual-generator electrical system.

4. Inspect an engine-driven generator or alternator.

5. Troubleshoot a voltage regulator in an aircraft electrical generating sytem.

6. Repair an engine direct-drive electric starter.

7. Troubleshoot a direct-drive electric starter system.

8. Inspect a turbine engine starter generator.

9. Install a generator on an engine specified by the examiner. Check the voltage output to determine whether or not it meets the manufacturer's specifications for voltage at a specified RPM.

10. Using an electrical system schematic diagram for a starter-generator installation, explain to the examiner the way the unit acts as a starter and then shifts into the function of a generator.

11. Install a tachometer generator and check its operation.

F02. Task: Install, Check, and Repair Engine Electrical Wiring, Controls, Switches, Indicators, and Protective Devices

Reference: AMT-P, Chapter 17

Typical Oral Questions

1. **What is used to protect a wire bundle from chafing where it passes through a hole in a bulkhead or frame?**
   A grommet around the edges of the hole.

2. **How are electrical wires protected where they pass through an area of high temperature?**
   Wires passing through these areas are insulated with high-temperature insulation, and the wires are enclosed in some type of protective conduit.

3. **What is the minimum separation allowed between a wire bundle and a fluid line that carries combustible fluid or oxygen?**
   Six inches.

4. **Which aircraft electrical circuit does not normally contain a fuse or circuit breaker?**
   The starter motor circuit.

5. **What is a starter-generator?**
   A single, engine-mounted component that serves as a starter for starting the turbine engine. When the engine is running, the circuitry automatically shifts so it acts as a compound-wound generator.

6. **When should aircraft wiring be installed in a conduit?**
   When the wiring passes through an area in the aircraft where open wiring could likely be damaged, such as through a wheel well.

7. **What is meant by a trip-free circuit breaker?**
   A circuit breaker that opens a circuit any time an excessive amount of current flows, regardless of the position of the circuit breaker's operating handle.

8. **Which way should the toggle of a switch that controls the propeller pitch move to place the propeller in low pitch (high RPM)?**
   Forward.

9. **Why are protective covers placed over some switches in an aircraft electrical circuit?**
   To prevent the switch from being inadvertently actuated.

Area of Operation: G. Lubrication Systems

G01. Task: Identify and Select Lubricants

Reference: AMT-P, Chapters 3 and 11

Typical Oral Questions

1. **What is straight mineral oil?**

   It is the lubricating oil as obtained by fractional distillation of crude oil. It does not have any additives.

2. **What is ashless dispersant (AD) oil?**

   A mineral lubricating oil containing additives that disperse the contaminants throughout the oil so they will not clump and clog oil passages. There are no ash-forming additives in AD oil.

3. **What is synthetic oil?**

   A lubricating oil that is made by chemically changing the nature of an oil base to give it the needed characteristics. Synthetic oil is the primary oil for turbine engines.

4. **Is automotive oil suitable for use in aircraft engines?**

   No, automotive and aviation oils are formulated for entirely different operating conditions.

5. **What is meant by a multiviscosity oil?**

   It is a lubricating oil with a viscosity index improver that increases the viscosity of the oil when it is hot and decreases the viscosity when it is cold.

6. **What are six functions of the oil in an aircraft engine?**
   a. *Reduces friction.*
   b. *Seals and cushions.*
   c. *Removes heat.*
   d. *Cleans inside the engine.*
   e. *Protects against corrosion.*
   f. *Performs hydraulic action.*

7. **Where can you find the grade of engine oil specified for a particular aircraft?**
   In the Aircraft Flight Manual or the Pilot's Operating Handbook for the aircraft.

G02. Task: Inspect, Check, Service, Troubleshoot, and Repair Engine Lubrications Systems

Reference: AMT-P, Chapters 3 and 11

Typical Oral Questions

1. **What components in a reciprocating-engine lubrication system must be inspected on a 100-hour or annual inspection?**
   The oil sump or tank, the oil strainer screen, the oil filter, the oil cooler and the temperature control valve, the oil pressure and temperature gages and any transmitters associated with them, and the entire engine for indication of oil leaks.

2. **What two instruments show the condition of a reciprocating-engine lubrication system?**
   Oil pressure and oil temperature gages.

3. **What must be done to an oil filter when it is removed from the engine?**
   It should be cut open and the pleated element examined to determine the type and amount of contaminant carried by the oil.

4. **What is a spectrometric oil analysis program?**
   A program in which a sample of oil is taken from the engine at regular intervals and sent to a laboratory, where it is burned in an electric arc. The resulting light is analyzed for the wavelengths of the elements that are present in the oil sample. Traces of aluminum, copper, and iron in the oil indicate wear of the pistons or wrist pin plugs (aluminum), cylinder walls or piston rings (iron), main bearings or bushings (copper). A single sample is meaningless. There must be a series of samples taken at regular intervals to measure the change in the amounts of these metals.

5. **What is the purpose of an air-oil separator, or deaerator, in a turbine engine oil tank?**

   In normal operation, the oil picks up a quantity of air and it is swirled as it enters the deaerator. The swirling action releases the air from the oil, and the air is used to pressurize the oil tank.

6. **What type of oil quantity indicator is used in most aircraft engines?**

   A dipstick that measures the quantity of oil in the tank or sump.

7. **When should the engine oil quantity be checked on a turbine engine?**

   As soon as practical after the engine is shut down.

8. **Where is the oil temperature measured on a reciprocating engine?**

   Usually at the oil pressure screen before the oil goes into the engine passages.

9. **How is oil pressure regulated in an aircraft engine?**

   A pressure-relief valve senses the desired pressure and sends all of the oil that caused excessive pressure back into the engine sump.

10. **Why do engine manufacturers recommend that engine lubricating oil be changed at specific intervals?**

    The oil picks up contaminants and carries them through the engine where they can cause wear. The oil also becomes acidic and causes corrosion in the engine.

11. **What is the purpose of the restricted orifice in the line between the oil pressure gage and the engine?**

    The restricted fitting helps dampen any pulsations in the oil pressure caused by the pump.

12. **What is a hot-tank lubrication system for a turbojet engine?**

    A lubrication system in which the oil cooler is in the pressure subsystem and the scavenged oil is not cooled before it is returned to the tank.

13. **What is a cold-tank lubrication system for a turbojet engine?**

    A lubrication system in which the oil cooler is in the scavenge subsystem, and the scavenged oil is cooled before it is returned to the tank.

Typical Practical Projects

1. Service the lubrication system in a turbine engine specified by the examiner. Choose the correct oil and explain the way the oil quantity is indicated.

2. Using a diagram of a turbine-engine lubrication system, identify the filters, the spray nozzles, the pumps, the relief valves, the check valves, and the bypass valves.

3. Demonstrate the way to take a sample of oil for a spectrometric oil analysis.

4. Demonstrate to the examiner the proper way to change the oil filter on an aircraft engine. Inspect the used filter for contamination and explain to the examiner the source of the contaminants. Explain the precautions that must be taken to avoid damaging the engine when installing the new filter.

5. Demonstrate the correct way to adjust the oil pressure on an engine specified by the examiner.

6. Demonstrate the correct way to preoil an engine specified by the examiner.

7. Using a list of oils approved for an aircraft engine, choose the correct oil for the existing climatic conditions and explain to the examiner the reason for your choice.

8. Using the Type Certificate Data Sheets for an aircraft specified by the examiner, find the oil quantity specified and the amount of undrainable oil that is trapped in the system.

9. Using the proper documentation for an engine specified by the examiner, locate the part number for the oil cooler. Describe the proper way to remove and replace the cooler, and prepare the engine for return to service including testing for leaks.

10. Replace a gasket or seal in the lubrication system of an engine specified by the examiner. Run the engine and check the entire system for leaks. Correct any leaks found.

11. Check the engine oil pressure.

12. Troubleshoot an engine oil pressure malfunction.

13. Troubleshoot an engine oil temperature system.

H01. Task: Inspect, Troubleshoot, and Repair Reciprocating and Turbine Engine Ignition Systems

Reference: AMT-P, Chapters 8 and 13

Typical Oral Questions

1. **What is the main advantage of a magneto ignition system over a battery ignition system for an aircraft reciprocating engine?**

   A magneto has its own source of electrical energy, and is not dependent upon the battery.

2. **What is the function of the capacitor in a magneto?**

   The capacitor minimizes arcing at the breaker points, and it speeds up the collapse of the primary current as the breaker points open.

3. **What happens in a magneto ignition system when the ignition switch is placed in the Off position?**

   The primary circuit is connected to ground.

4. **What is checked when a magneto is internally timed?**

   Internally timing a magneto consists of adjusting the breaker points so they will open at the instant the rotating magnet is in its E-gap position, and the distributor rotor is in position to direct the high voltage to cylinder number one.

5. **In what position should the ignition switch be placed when using a timing light on the magnetos?**

   In the Both position.

6. **What type of ignition system is used on most turbine engines?**

   High-intensity, intermittent-duty, capacitor discharge ignition systems.

7. **What is the E-gap in magneto timing?**

   The E-gap angle is the position of the rotating magnet when the primary current flowing in the magneto coil is the greatest. The breaker points open when the rotating magnet is in its E-gap position.

8. **What is the function of an impulse coupling?**

   An impulse coupling is a spring-driven coupling between the magneto and the engine. When the engine is being started, the impulse coupling holds the rotating magnet until the piston passes over its top center position and starts down. The impulse coupling releases the magnet and the spring spins it fast so that it produces a hot and late spark.

9. **How many igniters are used with most turbine engines?**

   Two.

10. What are two types of ignition systems used in turbine engines?

High-voltage systems and low-voltage systems.

11. With which type of turbine-engine ignition system is a glow plug igniter used?

A low-voltage system.

12. How is the strength of the magnet in a magneto checked?

The magneto is put on a test stand and rotated at a specified speed. The breaker points are held open and the primary current is measured. The strength of the magnet determines the amount of primary current.

13. In what position is the magnet in a magneto, when the greatest change in flux density in the coil core takes place?

It is a few degrees beyond its neutral position. When it is in this position, the breaker points open and the primary current is interrupted. The flux change in the coil core is the greatest.

14. In what position is the magnet in a magneto when the breaker points begin to open?

In its E-gap position, just a few degrees beyond its neutral position.

15. What malfunction in the ignition system would cause an aircraft reciprocating engine to continue to run after the ignition switch is placed in the Off position?

The ignition switch is not grounding the magneto primary circuit.

16. What kind of equipment is used to test an ignition harness for a reciprocating engine?

A high-voltage electrical leakage detector.

17. What is an All-Weather spark plug?

A shielded spark plug that has a recess in the shielding in which a resilient grommet on the ignition lead forms a watertight seal.

18. What is meant by the reach of a spark plug?

The length of the threads on the spark plug that screw into the cylinder head.

19. What is the difference between a hot spark plug and a cold spark plug?

A hot spark plug has a long path for the heat to travel between the nose core insulator and the spark plug shell. In a cold spark plug, the heat has a shorter distance to travel, and the spark plug operates cooler than a hot spark plug.

20. What is the advantage of fine-wire spark plugs over massive electrode spark plugs?

Fine-wire spark plugs have a firing end that is more open than that of a massive electrode spark plug. The open firing end allows the gases that contain lead to be purged from the spark plug so they will not form solid lead contaminates.

21. **Why is it important that the spark plugs be kept in numbered holes in a tray when they are removed from an engine?**

Spark plugs tell a good deal about the internal condition of the cylinders from which they were taken. By knowing the cylinder from which each spark plug came, the mechanic can take the proper action when a spark plug indicates such conditions as detonation or overheating.

22. **Why is it important that a torque wrench always be used when installing spark plugs in an aircraft engine?**

If the spark plugs are not put in tight enough, there is the possibility of a poor seal; if they are put in too tight, there is danger of cracking the insulation.

23. **What kind of gage should be used to measure the electrode gap in aircraft spark plugs?**

A round wire gage.

Typical Practical Projects

1. Replace and adjust a set of breaker points in a magneto specified by the examiner.

2. Internally time a magneto and install it on an engine specified by the examiner.

3. Clean and gap a spark plug specified by the examiner. Test it and explain to the examiner the reason a spark plug will function properly in an engine if it sparks properly in the tester.

4. Check the P-lead in a reciprocating engine ignition system. Explain the reason you cannot kill the engine with the magneto switch if the P-lead is broken.

5. Using the appropriate documentation, find the correct part number for the coil used in a magneto specified by the examiner.

6. Remove and inspect a low-voltage igniter plug from a turbine engine. Explain to the examiner the way the plug would be cleaned, tested, and replaced.

7. Describe the correct way to remove the exciter box from a turbine engine specified by the examiner. Explain the safety procedures that must be observed.

8. Demonstrate the correct way to inspect the ignition system of a turbine engine specified by the examiner.

H02. Task: Inspect, Troubleshoot, and Repair Turbine Engine Electrical Starting Systems

Reference: AMT-P, Chapter 13

Typical Oral Questions

1. **What kind of electric starting system is used on many of the smaller turbine engines?**

   A starter-generator.

2. **What happens when the start switch for a turbine engine with a starter-generator is placed in the START position?**

   a. *Current flows into the starter relay which closes and actuates the ignition exciter.*

   b. *Current flows through the series motor coils of the starter generator and rotates the engine until it starts.*

3. **What happens when the start switch for a turbine engine with a starter-generator is placed in the RUN position?**

   a. *The starter relay opens, shutting off current to the ignition exciter and the motor windings in the starter-generator.*

   b. *The generator field relay is closed connecting the voltage regulator to the starter-generator.*

   c. *The output of the generator flows to the bus through the generator circuit breaker.*

4. **What is indicated if the starter relay chatters rather than locks in, when the start switch is placed in the START position?**

   The battery voltage is too low to supply enough current to hold the relay engaged.

Typical Practical Projects

1. Demonstrate to the examiner the correct way to inspect an electrical turbine engine starter for proper operation.

2. Explain to the examiner the way a starter-generator starts a turbine engine and then shifts its action to that of a generator.

3. Inspect an electric turbine-engine starter and explain to the examiner the way it should be lubricated.

4. Demonstrate the way the brushes should be replaced in a starter-generator specified by the examiner.

H03. Task: Inspect, Service and Troubleshoot Turbine Engine Pneumatic Starting Systems

Reference: AMT-P, Chapter 13

Typical Oral Questions

1. **Why are air-turbine starters superior to electric starters for large turbine engines?**

   They are light weight for the torque they produce.

2. **Where does an air-turbine starter get its air for starting the engines on a jet transport airplane?**

   From an APU, GPU, or from a running engine.

3. **What is the purpose of the shear section in an air-turbine drive shaft?**

   If the ratchet mechanism fails to release and the engine drives the starter to a speed higher than its design speed, the shear section will break and disconnect the starter from the engine.

4. **What prevents too high an air pressure from overspeeding an air-turbine starter?**

   The air shutoff and regulating valve.

5. **Where does an air-turbine starter get it lubricating oil?**

   It has a self-contained lubrication system with the oil held in the starter housing.

6. **What device in an air-turbine starter warns a technician if there are any metal chips or particles in the oil?**

   Magnetic chip detectors warn of any metal contamination in the oil.

Typical Practical Projects

1. Disassemble, identify components, and reassemble a magneto.

2. Inspect the magneto breaker points.

3. Test the high-tension leads.

4. Remove and install an ignition harness.

5. Check a magneto on a test bench.

6. Check the serviceability of the condensers.

Continued

---

7. Check the ignition coils.

8. Check the ignition leads.

9. Install and/or time a magneto on an engine.

10. Troubleshoot a turbine or reciprocating engine ignition system.

11. Troubleshoot a turbine engine's igniters.

12. Inspect the turbine engine ignition system.

13. Fabricate an ignition lead.

Area of Operation: I. Fuel Metering Systems

I01. Task: Troubleshoot and Adjust Turbine Engine Fuel Metering Systems and Electronic Engine Fuel Controls

Reference: AMT-P, Chapter 12

Typical Oral Questions

1. **What parameters are normally sensed by a turbine-engine fuel control?**
   a. *Power lever angle.*
   b. *Compressor inlet total temperature.*
   c. *Compressor RPM.*
   d. *Burner pressure.*

2. **What is meant by trimming a turbine engine?**
   Adjusting the fuel control for the proper specific gravity of the fuel and for the proper idle and full throttle RPM.

3. **What are two types of electronic fuel controls for turbine engines?**
   Supervisory Electronic Engine Control and Full-Authority Digital Electronic Control.

4. **What is a FADEC?**
   A Full-Authority Digital Electronic Control (FADEC) is a high-precision digital electronic fuel control that functions during all engine operations. It includes the Electronic Engine Control (EEC) and functions with the Flight Management Computer (FMC) to measure the fuel to the nozzles in such a way that prevents overshooting of power changes and over-temperature conditions. FADEC furnishes information to the Engine Indication and Crew Alerting System (EICAS).

5. Does a turbine engine controlled by a FADEC require manual trimming?

No, this is done by the FADEC.

6. When should a turbine engine be retrimmed?

Any time there is a decrease in engine thrust, and after any maintenance that the manufacturer specifies as requiring retrimming.

7. Are the instruments installed in an aircraft suitable for use when trimming a turbine engine?

No, a special analyzer/trimmer such as a JetCal should be used.

8. What specifications are used to trim a turbine engine?

The data plate specifications for the specific engine. This data was obtained when the engine was calibrated in the manufacturer's test cell.

9. Where should ambient temperature be measured when trimming a turbine engine?

In a shaded area as near the engine inlet as is practical.

Typical Practical Projects

1. Identify the components of a carburetor.

2. Identify the main discharge nozzle in a pressure carburetor.

3. Service a carburetor fuel inlet screen.

4. Interpret a diagram showing fuel and air flow through a float-type and/or a pressure type carburetor.

5. Remove and/or install a main metering jet in a carburetor.

6. Identify, remove, and/or install a float-type carburetor.

7. Inspect a float needle and/or seat in a float-type carburetor.

8. Remove and/or install the mixture control system in a float-type carburetor.

9. Check the float level on a float-type carburetor.

10. Remove and/or install the accelerating pump in a float-type carburetor.

11. Identify a carburetor's air-bleed system.

Continued

Typical Practical Projects *Continued*

12. Adjust the idle speed and/or mixture.

13. Describe the conditions that may cause slow acceleration in a pressure-type carburetor engine.

14. Describe the conditions that may result in turbine engine RPM overspeed.

15. Describe the conditions that may result in malfunctions in a pressure-injection carburetor fuel regulator unit.

16. Replace a direct-injection fuel nozzle.

17. Inspect a turbine fuel control unit.

18. Remove, inspect, and install a turbine engine fuel nozzle.

19. Set or position fuel metering cockpit controls for engine start.

Area of Operation: J. Engine Fuel Systems

J01. Task: Inspect, Check, Troubleshoot, and Repair Reciprocating and Turbine Engine Fuel Systems

Reference: AMT-P, Chapters 4 and 12

Typical Oral Questions

1. **What is meant by a compensated fuel pump?**

   It is a fuel pump that senses the ambient air pressure and maintains the fuel pressure a specific amount above this air pressure.

2. **What would likely cause a reciprocating engine equipped with a float carburetor to hesitate momentarily when the throttle is rapidly advanced from idle to full power?**

   A malfunctioning accelerator pump.

3. **What is the function of a float carburetor?**

   The float carburetor's function is to measure airflow through the engine induction system and dispense the appropriate amount of gasoline into the airflow for all engine operating perimeters and conditions. It must also provide the fuel in a state that is as vaporized as possible by the time ignition occurs in the engine cylinders.

4. **Why do aircraft fuel metering systems for reciprocating engines have mixture controls?**

   The air density decreases as the aircraft ascends, causing the mixture to become richer. The mixture control allows the fuel to be decreased to maintain a fuel-air mixture ratio that produces the desired power.

5. **What are the two types of fuel injection systems used on modern reciprocating aircraft engines?**

   Teledyne Continental (TCM) system and Precision Airmotive (Bendix) system.

6. **What is used in the TCM fuel injection system to control the amount of fuel sent to the nozzles?**

   The engine speed determines the injector pump output pressure. The relief valve determines the fuel for low-speed operation, and the adjustable orifice determines the fuel for high-speed operation.

7. **What is used in the Precision Airmotive system to control the amount of fuel sent to the nozzles?**

   The mass of the air entering the engine acts on an air diaphragm that controls a servo ball valve in the line between the regulator and the flow divider.

8. **Where are the fuel strainers normally located in an aircraft fuel system?**

   Finger strainers are located in the tank outlet, the main strainer, located at the lowest point in the fuel system, and strainers in the carburetor or fuel injection system.

9. **What are two types of fuel heaters used in a jet transport aircraft?**

   Air-to-fuel and oil-to-fuel heat exchangers.

10. **What kind of fuel boost pumps are normally installed inside the fuel tanks?**

    Centrifugal pumps.

11. **What two things are adjusted when setting the idling conditions on a float carburetor?**

    a. *Idling RPM by adjusting the throttle stop.*
    b. *Idling mixture by adjusting idle needle valve.*

12. **What are three functions of the boost pump in the tank of a jet transport aircraft?**

    a. *To pressurize the fuel in the line between the tank and the engine-driven pump.*
    b. *To transfer fuel from one tank to another to balance the fuel load.*
    c. *To pump fuel from the tank into the dump chute when fuel is being dumped.*

Typical Practical Projects

1. Explain to the examiner the way you can tell when a fuel strainer for a turbine engine has been bypassed.

2. Explain to the examiner the way to check a remotely located fuel selector valve for proper operation and freedom of action.

3. Demonstrate the correct way to remove and clean a main fuel filter and check it for leaks after it has been reinstalled.

4. Demonstrate the correct way to check a fuel boost pump to determine that it is putting out the pressure specified in the aircraft maintenance manual.

5. Identify to the examiner the components in the fuel system of a reciprocating or turbine-powered aircraft.

6. Remove and/or install an engine-driven fuel pump.

7. Rig a remotely operated fuel valve.

8. Demonstrate the way to inspect the fuel nozzle on a turbine engine for the correct spray pattern.

9. Check the fuel boost pumps for correct pressure.

10. Remove and/or install a fuel boost pump.

11. Locate and identify a turbine engine fuel heater.

12. Check the fuel pressure warning light function.

13. Inspect the engine fuel system fluid lines and/or components.

14. Troubleshoot abnormal fuel pressure.

15. Troubleshoot a turbine engine fuel heater system.

16. Remove, clean, and/or replace an engine fuel strainer.

17. Troubleshoot engine fuel pressure fluctuation.

18. Inspect the fuel selector valve.

19. Locate and identify the fuel selector placards.

Area of Operation: K. Induction and Engine Airflow Systems
K01. Task: Inspect, Check, Troubleshoot, and Repair Engine Ice Systems

Reference: AMT-P, Chapter 4

Typical Oral Questions

1. **Why does ice form in the throat of a float carburetor?**

   When liquid fuel evaporates it absorbs enough heat from the air to cause moisture to condense out and freeze.

2. **Does the application of carburetor heat cause the fuel-air mixture to become richer or leaner?**

   The less dense, heated air draws the same amount of fuel from the carburetor as cold air, therefore the mixture becomes richer.

3. **What happens to engine RPM when carburetor heat is applied?**

   The RPM drops.

4. **Why should the use of carburetor heat be limited when operating an engine with the aircraft on the ground?**

   The air that flows into the engine when carburetor heat is applied is not filtered.

5. **Why is a fuel-injected reciprocating engine not as prone to icing as an engine equipped with a float carburetor?**

   In a fuel-injected engine, the liquid fuel evaporates in the intake valve chamber of the hot cylinder head.

6. **How is ice prevented from forming on the nose cowl, nose dome and inlet guide vanes of a turbine engine?**

   Hot compressor bleed air flows through passages in these components to keep them too warm for ice to form.

Typical Practical Projects

1. Demonstrate the correct way to check for proper functioning of a carburetor heat system on an operating engine.

2. Demonstrate the correct way to inspect a carburetor heat system for proper movement of the air valve, and proper cushion on the control.

3. Identify the components in the anti-icing system in a turbine engine installation specified by the examiner.

Continued

---

4. Explain to the examiner the probable locations of induction ice.

5. Identify to the examiner the turbine engine air intake ice protected areas.

6. Troubleshoot an engine that idles poorly.

7. Troubleshoot an engine that fails to start.

8. Troubleshoot a carburetor heat system.

K02. Task: Inspect, Check, and Repair Carburetor Air Intake, Induction Manifolds

Reference: AMT-P, Chapter 4

Typical Oral Questions

1. **What does a fuel-injected engine have that prevents the loss of induction air, if the air inlet filter should become covered with ice?**

   An alternate air valve allows warm air from inside the engine cowling to flow into the fuel metering system.

2. **What would be the effect on engine operation of an air leak in the intake pipe for one cylinder?**

   That cylinder would run lean and detonation could occur.

3. **Why is it very important that the induction air filters be kept clean and replaced as often as the manufacturer recommends?**

   Clogged air filters can restrict the air entering the engine.

Typical Practical Projects

1. Demonstrate the correct way to clean an induction air filter specified by the examiner.

2. Demonstrate the correct way to check an induction system for air leaks.

3. Inspect an induction system for obstruction.

4. Demonstrate how to correct a leak in an intake pipe to a cylinder.

5. Identify the components in the intake side of a turbocharged engine specified by the examiner.

6. Check a turbocharger for operation.

Area of Operation: L. Engine Cooling Systems

L01. Task: Inspect, Check, Troubleshoot, and Repair Engine Cooling Systems

Reference: AMT-P, Chapters 7 and 11

Typical Oral Questions

1. **What is meant by pressure cooling of an air-cooled engine?**
   Ram air on one side of the engine is forced by a series of baffles to flow through the fins on the cylinders to a low-pressure area on the other side of the engine.

2. **What must be inspected on the cooling system of an air-cooled engine?**
   All of the baffles and air seals must be in place and in good condition.

3. **Why should an air-cooled engine not be run up to high power without the cowling installed?**
   The engine depends on the cowling to force air through the cylinder fins to remove the excess heat.

4. **Why do some air-cooled engine installations have cowl flaps?**
   Cowl flaps produce a low pressure on one side of the engine to pull air through the cooling fins on the cylinders.

5. **Where can you find what is the maximum amount of cylinder fin area that can be removed in order to clean out a damaged area?**
   In the engine overhaul manual.

6. What document describes the proper use of cowl flaps on an air-cooled engine?
The Pilot's Operating Handbook.

Typical Practical Projects

1. Demonstrate the correct way to inspect the cooling system of an engine specified by the examiner.

2. Demonstrate the correct way to inspect a cowl flap installation and explain the way to adjust it.

3. Explain to the examiner the function of the baffles and seals in an engine compartment.

4. Repair a cylinder head baffle.

5. Repair a cylinder cooling fin.

6. Identify the location of turbine engine insulation blankets.

7. Identify the turbine engine cooling air flow.

8. Troubleshoot an engine cooling system.

9. Identify the exhaust augmentor cooled engine components.

10. Repair the turbine engine insulation blankets.

11. Identify the rotorcraft engine cooling components.

12. Troubleshoot a rotorcraft engine's cooling system.

13. Inspect a rotorcraft engine's cooling system.

14. Inspect an engine exhaust augmentor cooling system.

M01. Task: Inspect, Check, Troubleshoot, and Repair Engine Exhaust, Heat Exchangers, and Turbocharger Systems

Reference: AMT-P, Chapters 6 and 14

Typical Oral Questions

1. **How does a leak appear in an engine exhaust system?**

   It normally looks like a gray or black feather-shaped streak coming from a crack or from a location where components are not in perfect alignment.

2. **How can you check an exhaust system for leaks?**

   Pressurize the exhaust system with the discharge from a vacuum cleaner and wipe a soap solution over all joints and suspect areas. A leak will cause bubbles to form.

3. **How do the components in the exhaust system of a turbocharged engine allow for expansion and contraction due to heat, and at the same time prevent leakage?**

   Bellows and ball joints prevent leakage while allowing contraction and expansion.

4. **What type of damage is most common in the exhaust system of a reciprocating engine?**

   Cracks caused by expansion and contraction.

5. **Should a turbocharged engine be started with the waste gate open or closed?**

   Open, so as much exhaust as possible will bypass the turbine.

Typical Practical Projects

1. Demonstrate the correct way to inspect a reciprocating engine exhaust system for leaks.

2. Identify for the examiner the components in a turbocharger system, and explain the way the system operates.

3. Inspect the wastegate and the controller for a turbocharged engine and explain the way the controller changes the wastegate position.

4. Demonstrate the proper way to replace exhaust gaskets on an engine specified by the examiner. Explain the precautions that must be taken when working on the exhaust system.

5. Identify the type of exhaust system on a particular aircraft.

Continued

Typical Practical Projects *Continued*

6. Clean the exhaust system components.

7. Inspect an exhaust system's internal baffles or diffusers.

8. Remove and install the exhaust ducts.

9. Inspect an exhaust heat exchanger.

10. Remove and install a heat exchanger collector tube.

11. Perform a heat exchanger collector tube leak test.

12. Inspect a turbine engine exhaust nozzle.

13. Troubleshoot an exhaust muffler heat exchanger.

14. Repair an exhaust system leak.

15. Demonstrate the way to mark an exhaust component for repair. Explain why lead pencils should not be used for marking.

M02. Task: Troubleshoot and Repair Engine Thrust Reverser Systems and Related Components

Reference: AMT-P, Chapters 6 and 14

Typical Oral Questions

1. **Why are thrust reversers not normally used when the airplane is moving below approximately 60 knots?**

   There is a danger of recirculating the exhaust gases, and of the engine ingesting foreign objects stirred up by the high-velocity gases.

2. **What is a mechanical-blockage thrust reverser?**

   A thrust reverser that slides a pair of scoop-shaped doors aft and opens them so they block the rearward flow of gases and deflect the gases forward.

3. **How does a cascade-type thrust reverser operate?**

   A portion of the fan cowl moves rearward, and a series of blocker doors deflect the fan discharge air through fan cascades that direct the discharge air forward. At the same time, blocker doors shut off the flow of gases from the core engine and deflect it through cascades that direct it forward.

Typical Practical Projects

1. Demonstrate to the examiner the way a thrust reverser operates.

2. Explain to the examiner the way to check the thrust reverser for security of mounting and for cracks or other forms of heat damage.

3. Explain to the examiner the repairs that can be made to a thrust reverser.

4. Troubleshoot a thrust reverser system.

Area of Operation: N. Propellers

N01. Task: Inspect, Check, and Repair Propeller Synchronizing and Ice Control Systems

Reference: AMT-P, Chapter 19

Typical Oral Questions

1. **What is meant by a slave engine with regard to propeller synchronization?**

   This is the engine in a multi-engine airplane whose RPMs follow those set on the master engine.

2. **What does the pilot do to change the RPM of an engine equipped with a constant-speed propeller when it is operating within the constant-speed range?**

   The pilot moves the propeller pitch control. This changes the compression on the speeder spring inside the governor which moves the pilot valve. The pilot valve directs oil into or out of the propeller to change the pitch of the blades. The change in pitch changes the air load on the propeller which changes the RPM.

3. **How is ice prevented from forming on propeller blades?**

   A chemical anti-icing system is used. A mixture of isopropyl alcohol and ethylene glycol is pumped into a slinger ring on the back of the propeller hub. From there centrifugal force slings it out along the blades. Ice cannot form on the resulting slick surface.

4. **How is ice removed from propeller blades?**

   An electrothermal deicing system is used. Electrical heating elements are embedded in rubber boots that are bonded to the leading edges of the blades. Low-voltage DC flows from the propeller deicer control through brushes and slip rings to the heating elements. The timer sends current to one propeller for about 90 seconds and then to the other for the next 90 seconds. This allows the ice to form and then break loose and blow away.

5. **How can you determine that the electrically heated deicer boots on the propeller blades are working as they should?**

Observe the loadmeter or ammeter to see if the proper current is flowing, and follow the sequence of boot heating by feeling with your hands to see which one is heating. The boots should all have a similar heat rise in the same length of time.

6. **How are propellers on a twin-engine airplane synchronized?**

The propeller governor of the master engine is set to the desired RPM. A signal from the master engine governor is sent to the control box which sends a signal to a stepping motor. This motor adjusts the propeller governor and fuel control of the slave engine causing it to maintain exactly the same RPM as the master engine.

Typical Practical Projects

1. Demonstrate to the examiner the way to check and replace the brushes for an electrothermal propeller deicer.

2. Demonstrate the correct way to check for proper operation of a propeller electrothermal deicer system.

3. Demonstrate the way to check a propeller synchronizing system to determine whether or not it is holding the RPM of the two engines within the allowable tolerance.

4. Troubleshoot a thrust reverser system.

5. Troubleshoot a turboprop propeller system.

6. Repair an anti-icing or de-icing system on a propeller.

7. Perform a 100-hour inspection on a propeller.

N02. Task: Identify and Select Propeller Lubricants

Reference: AMT-P, Chapter 19

Typical Oral Question

1. **Where do you find a list of the lubricants that are approved for use in a constant-speed propeller?**

In the maintenance manual for the propeller.

---

1. Describe the operation of a propeller.

2. Select the proper lubricant for a propeller as specified by the propeller manufacturer.

3. Demonstrate to the examiner the correct way to lubricate a propeller. Use the proper reference materials to find the lubricants that are to be used.

N03. Task: Inspect, Check, Service, and Repair Fixed-Pitch, Constant-Speed and Feathering Propellers, and Propeller Governing Systems

Reference: AMT-P, Chapter 19

Typical Oral Questions

1. **Who, or what facility, is authorized to perform major repairs to a propeller?**
   An FAA-approved propeller repair station that is authorized for the specific propeller.

2. **What checks and maintenance is a mechanic with a powerplant rating allowed to make on a propeller?**
   - *Check the track of the propeller blades.*
   - *Remove small nicks and scratches from the blades.*
   - *Check the dynamic balance of a propeller.*
   - *Lubricate the propeller.*

3. **What adjustment can a mechanic with a powerplant rating make to a propeller governor?**
   Adjust the maximum RPM stop.

4. **Why do some aircraft engines have a critical range of operation?**
   The engine and propeller combination have a resonant frequency problem in which excessive vibration can occur in a certain range of RPM. The tachometer for an aircraft with this limitation is marked with a red arc. When it is necessary to pass through this range it must be done as quickly as practical.

5. **What is the difference between a controllable propeller and a constant-speed propeller?**
   Basically, it is the control system. A controllable-pitch propeller uses a manually operated oil valve to control the pitch, and a constant-speed propeller uses a governor to control the valve.

6. **Does centrifugal twisting moment on a propeller blade tend to move the blades toward high pitch or toward low pitch?**

   Toward low pitch.

7. **Do the counterweights on a propeller tend to move the blades toward high pitch or toward low pitch?**

   Toward high pitch.

8. **What is adjusted inside the governor for a constant-speed propeller to change the speed at which the propeller is operating?**

   The compression of the speeder spring.

9. **What is the function of the accumulator used with some McCauley feathering propellers?**

   The accumulator stores oil under pressure when the engine is operating normally. This oil is used to help the propeller blades move toward low pitch when the propeller is being unfeathered.

10. **What is meant by the beta range of operation of a turboprop propeller?**

    This is the mode of ground operation, and it includes starting, taxiing, and ground reverse operation.

11. **What is meant by the alpha range of operation of a turboprop propeller?**

    This is the in-flight mode of operation from takeoff to landing.

12. **What is done to cause a McCauley propeller to feather?**

    Oil is allowed to drain out of the propeller.

13. **What keeps a McCauley feathering propeller from feathering when the engine is shutdown on the ground?**

    A spring-loaded latch mechanism prevents the blades moving into the feather position when the engine is shut down on the ground. In the air, aerodynamic forces keep the propeller rotating fast enough that centrifugal force holds the blades unlatched so they can move to the feather position when oil pressure is taken out of the propeller.

14. **Should an adjustable-pitch propeller be in high pitch or in low pitch for takeoff?**

    In low pitch.

15. **What is done to cause a Hydromatic propeller to feather?**

    High-pressure engine oil is directed into the propeller through the governor.

16. **When making a magneto check on an engine equipped with a constant-speed propeller, should the propeller control be in the low-pitch or the high-pitch position?**

    It should be in the low-pitch, high RPM position.

Typical Practical Projects

1. Using the correct reference material, find out if there is any RPM range that is restricted for an engine-propeller combination specified by the examiner.

2. Describe the operation of a propeller.

3. Inspect a wooden propeller metal tipping.

4. Perform a 100-hour inspection on a propeller.

N04. Task: Install, Troubleshoot, and Remove Propellers

Reference: AMT-P, Chapter 19

Typical Oral Questions

1. **What can be done to prevent the front cone from bottoming when installing a propeller on a splined shaft?**
   Install a spacer behind the rear cone to move the propeller forward on the shaft.

2. **What is the function of the snap ring inside the hub of a propeller that is mounted on a tapered or splined shaft?**
   The snap ring allows the propeller to be pulled off of the shaft when the retaining nut is backed off.

3. **Why is a propeller indexed to the engine crankshaft?**
   The relationship between the propeller and the engine crankshaft is chosen to produce the minimum vibration.

4. **What instrument is used to measure the blade angle of a propeller?**
   A universal propeller protractor.

5. **Where is the propeller protractor placed to measure the propeller blade angle?**
   At a distance from the center of the propeller hub. This distance is specified in the propeller maintenance manual in terms of propeller blade stations.

Typical Practical Projects

1. Remove and replace a fixed-pitch propeller on an engine with a splined or tapered shaft. Explain the reason propellers are indexed to the crankshaft. Explain the reason for the snap ring in the propeller hub, and demonstrate the application of the proper torque to tighten the retaining nut. Explain what to do if the front cone bottoms when the propeller is reinstalled.

2. Remove and replace a constant-speed propeller on an engine specified by the examiner.

3. Demonstrate the use of a universal propeller protractor to measure the blade angle of a propeller specified by the examiner. Explain the reason for choosing the position to place the protractor.

4. Perform a check of tip tracking a metal fixed-pitch propeller. Explain to the examiner the correct way to correct a minor out-of-track condition.

5. Remove a spinner from a constant-speed propeller and check the spinner bulkhead for cracks. Explain the proper type of repair to a cracked bulkhead. Explain the precautions that must be taken when reinstalling the spinner.

6. Locate the procedures for balancing a fixed-pitch propeller.

7. Remove, inspect, and/or install a propeller governor.

8. Adjust a propeller governor.

N05. Task: Inspection and Repair of Aluminum Alloy Propeller Blades

Reference: AMT-P, Chapter 19

Typical Oral Questions

1. **What is the extent of the repairs a mechanic with a powerplant rating can make to a propeller?**
   Only minor repairs or minor alterations.

2. **Where can examples of acceptable repairs to aluminum alloy propeller blades be found?**
   In AC 43.13-1B, Chapter 8, Section 4.

3. **Is it permissible to cold straighten a damaged aluminum alloy propeller blade to facilitate shipping it to a repair station?**
   No, this could cause hidden damage that may render the blade nonrepairable.

4. **What would be the classification of maintenance for shortening a propeller blade?**

   Major repair.

5. **May transverse cracks in a metal propeller blade be repaired?**

   No, a transverse crack of any size is reason for rejecting the blade.

6. **What damage to an aluminum alloy propeller blade can be repaired by a mechanic holding a powerplant rating?**

   Small roughness, nicks, and scratches in the leading edge of the blades.

7. **How are small nicks removed from the leading edge of a propeller blade?**

   File them out with a fine file or stone, leaving a smooth contour.

8. **Who is allowed to reduce the diameter of a type certificated propeller?**

   An FAA-certificated propeller repair station with approval for the particular propeller.

9. **How can you determine that a surface scratch in an aluminum alloy propeller blade is not actually a crack?**

   Clean the damage out to a saucer-shaped depression and spray the area with a dye-penetrant liquid. Allow it time to seep into a crack if one is present, then wipe all of the liquid off the surface. Spray the area with a developer. If the damage is actually a crack, the developer will pull the penetrant out and it will form a visible line.

Typical Practical Projects

1. Perform a dye-penetrant inspection to an area on an aluminum alloy propeller blade specified by the examiner.

2. Inspect a propeller for damage and perform a repair to remove small surface damage.

3. Clean an aluminum alloy propeller.

Area of Operation: O. Turbine-Powered Auxiliary Power Units

O01. Task: Inspect, Check, Service, and Troubleshoot Turbine-Driven Auxiliary Power Units

Reference: AMT-P, Chapter 13

Typical Oral Questions

1. **Where are most APUs located in modern jet transport aircraft?**

   In the tail cone of the fuselage.

---

2. What is the function of an APU?

An APU provides electric power and compressed air when the main engines are not operating.

3. What are two sources of compressed air from an APU?

From bleed air from the APU turbine compressor, or from a load compressor driven by a free turbine in the engine.

4. Where in maintenance information based on the ATA-100 system would you find instructions for inspecting and servicing the engine of an airborne APU?

In section 49 20.

5. How is most of the troubleshooting done for a modern APU?

By the fault codes generated by the FADEC.

6. What ensures that an APU will not be shut down while it is too hot?

The APU fuel control incorporates an automatic time-delay feature that closes the bleed air valve to remove most of the load and reduce the APU temperature before it is shut down.

7. What prevents the APU exceeding its safe operating limits when the bleed air valve is wide open?

The FADEC monitors the load and regulates the fuel going to the APU to prevent it from exceeding its safe limits.

8. What document would you use to find the safety procedures to follow when replacing an igniter plug in an APU engine?

The maintenance manual for the APU.